THE PERFECT MURDER

Peter James'

THE PERFECT MURDER

Written for the stage
by Shaun McKenna

JOSEF WEINBERGER PLAYS

LONDON

THE PERFECT MURDER
First published in 2015
by Josef Weinberger Ltd
12-14 Mortimer Street, London W1T 3JJ
www.josef-weinberger.com / plays@jwmail.co.uk

ISBN: 978 0 85676 348 9

Printed by Commercial Colour Press plc, Hainault, Essex

PETER JAMES

Peter James is one of the UK's most treasured crime and thriller novelists. His Roy Grace detective novels have sold over six million in the UK alone and 15 million worldwide in total, including being number one bestsellers in Russia, Germany, France and Canada. The series is now translated into 36 languages. Peter's Roy Grace novels have achieved seven consecutive number ones on *The Sunday Times* Bestseller lists, and in the autumn of 2012, *Not Dead Yet* toppled the 50 Shades trilogy off the number-one paperback fiction slot, ending its 25-week domination of the chart. His novella *The Perfect Murder* (2010) went straight in at number one in the iBooks chart and spent 40 consecutive weeks in the iBooks top 10.

An established film producer and scriptwriter, Peter was educated at Charterhouse, then at film school. He lived in North America for a number of years, working as a screenwriter and film producer, before returning to England. He has produced numerous films including *The Merchant of Venice,* starring Al Pacino, Jeremy Irons and Joseph Fiennes. Both a film and a television adaptation of the Roy Grace series is currently in development, with Peter overseeing all aspects, including the scriptwriting. In 2009, he was awarded an honorary doctorate by the University of Brighton in recognition of his services to literature and the community. Peter is co-patron of Neighbourhood Watch, nationwide; patron of Crimestoppers in Sussex, together with Dame Vera Lynn; patron of Brighton, Hove and District Samaritans, and patron of the Whitehawk Inn. In 2011, Peter was made chair of the Crime Writers' Association and served two consecutive terms. Peter has won many literary awards, including the publicly voted ITV3 Crime Thriller Awards' People's Bestseller Dagger in 2011, and he was shortlisted for the Wellcome Trust Book Prize for *Perfect People* in 2012. As popular internationally as in the UK, he won the US Barry Award for Best British Crime Novel, for *Dead Man's Grip* in the autumn of 2012.

SHAUN McKENNA

Shaun McKenna is an award-winning dramatist, screenwriter and lyricist. Shaun's acclaimed 2012 stage adaptation of *Ladies In Lavender* with Hayley Mills and Belinda Lang won five Broadway World UK awards including Best Regional Play. His theatre career began in the 1990s with three commissions from the Royal, Northampton – *How Green Was My Valley, To Serve Them All My Days* and an original play, *Ruling Passions*.

TV commissions include the two-part thriller *Cuckoo, The Crooked Man, Like Father Like Son*, three series of *Heartbeat* and *Doctors*. He wrote the recent documentary series *Great West End Theatres* on Sky Arts and has a six part espionage series in development with ITV.

Musical theatre credits include five West End musicals, including the forthcoming Glenn Miller show *Feelin' In The Mood*. Shaun co-wrote the 2007 stage version of *The Lord of the Rings* with director Matthew Warchus (SOBOM Outstanding Achievement Award, DORA Award Best Musical and Olivier Award Best Musical nomination). A new version of the show begins a world tour in 2015. His most recent musical *Last Dance* premiered off Broadway in September 2012. Shaun's earlier West End credits include *Maddie* in 1997 and *Lautrec* in 2000, written with Charles Aznavour. At the Edinburgh Festival hits have included *Only You Can Save Mankind* in 2005 based on a Terry Pratchett novel and *Murder Mystery Musical* in 2009. His acclaimed *Heidi Trilogy*, written with Stephen Keeling, ran in Switzerland and German between 2005-2008 and was nominated for the Prix Walo. Arena shows include *Ben Hur Live* which premiered at the O2 in 2009 and was revived in Rome in 2011. His new arena show, co-devised with Broadway director Philip Wm. McKinley, is *The Bible: In The Beginning*, set to premiere in the USA in 2016.

For more information visit www.shaunmckenna.net or follow him on Twitter @SMcKennawriter.

CHARACTERS

(in order of appearance)

Victor Smiley

Kamila Walcak

Joan Smiley

Detective Constable Roy Grace

Don Kirk

THE SETTING

The action of the play takes place in Victor and Joan's small 1960s house in Saltdean, outside Brighton, and in Kamila's room at the Kitten Parlour, a brothel in Brighton.

Kamila's room is small and cheaply furnished. Victor and Joan's house has the following elements:

A living room with a settee, a dining table and chairs and a sideboard. There is a large TV set but this is on the 'fourth wall' and therefore not visible to the audience.

From the living room, a doorway (without a door) leads to the kitchen, which contains the usual array of cupboards and appliances, and a chest freezer. A half-glazed back door and a window with a semi-transparent blind look out onto the garden.

Also from the living room, a door leads to a hallway and the rest of the house, unseen except for Victor and Joan's bedroom, upstairs.

THE PERFECT MURDER was first presented by Jass Productions and Peter James at the Orchard Theatre, Dartford on January 8th 2014, prior to a national UK tour. The cast was as follows:

VICTOR SMILEY	Les Dennis
KAMILA WALCAK	Simona Armstrong
JOAN SMILEY	Claire Goose
DC ROY GRACE	Steven Miller
DON KIRK	Gray O'Brien

Directed by Ian Talbot

Designed by Michael Holt

Lighting Design by Mark Howett

Sound Design by Martin Hodgso

Original Music composed by Laura Tisdall

ACT ONE

Scene One

Darkness.

VICTOR   My wife doesn't understand me.

(*A moment.*)

I'm going to kill her. I've been planning it for ages. Bit by bit by bit.

(*Through a thin curtain, fading light picks out a middle-aged man in bed. This is* VICTOR SMILEY.)

You think I'm kidding. All talk and no do. Well, let me tell you. I've got a bottle of cyanide in my garden shed. It's on the shelf with the weed killer and the oil for the mower. Sometimes I go down there and just stare at it.

(*Offstage, a toilet flushes,* KAMILA *enters. She is 20s, skinny, Croatian. She turns on the overhead light. We see we are in* KAMILA'S *poky room in the Kitten Parlour, a brothel.*)

KAMILA   Time is up.

VICTOR   That's not fair, you went to the loo.

KAMILA   Can't help that.

VICTOR   Five more minutes, eh? Come on, you owe me.

KAMILA   You must go or pay more.

VICTOR   But I've just been talking . . .

KAMILA   It's not me. Boss. Very strict.

VICTOR   Give me a kiss.

KAMILA	Kiss is extra, you know that. You are a good man, Victor.
VICTOR	Tell that to my wife.
KAMILA	You got passion.
VICTOR	Yes.
KAMILA	Important man. Rich.
VICTOR	(*laughs*) Not rich. IT Managers don't get rich.
KAMILA	Rich. (*Taps his head.*) Up here. Many ideas.
VICTOR	Plenty of those, yeah.
KAMILA	Wife should be glad.
VICTOR	But she isn't. That's why I'm going to kill her. Then we'll see who's a loser. (KAMILA *laughs.*) Don't laugh. (*A moment.*) Murder's my hobby.
KAMILA	You are a serial killer? Help.
	(*She giggles – then sees his face.*)
VICTOR	Don't laugh at me. It is my hobby.
KAMILA	Hey, relax. Victor, don't be angry. (*An idea.*) I know what you like.
	(*She climbs on the bed behind him, starts to massage his shoulders.*)
VICTOR	I've made a study of it.
KAMILA	Oh dear. Like rock.
VICTOR	I've got a list. Rule number one: Plan carefully. Number Four: Don't have a criminal record. Seventeen: Bloodstains are hard to remove completely. Twenty two: Act as if you're missing her. Twenty nine . . .

KAMILA	How many rules are there?
VICTOR	Fifty three. Killing Joan will be the perfect murder.
KAMILA	Ha! There is no such thing.
VICTOR	The cops can't solve a murder if they don't know it's a murder, can they? Not if it looks like an accident. I saw the Chief Constable on telly. He said, "The perfect murder is the one we never hear about."
KAMILA	You really think about this.
VICTOR	It's my specialist subject. I should go on Mastermind. (*Seeing she does not understand.*) The black leather chair.
KAMILA	You want leather?
VICTOR	What?
KAMILA	Like Fifty Shades?
VICTOR	Carry on. It's lovely. I'd visit you every day if I could.
KAMILA	You can. I will arrange.
VICTOR	I can't afford it. I don't suppose I could get a special rate?
KAMILA	I asked before. Boss said no.
VICTOR	(*with a sigh*) Pass my watch, then.
	(*She leans over to pick up his watch from the bedside table.*)
KAMILA	Nice watch. Real gold?
VICTOR	(*putting it on*) It was my Dad's. His pride and joy. You'd have liked my Dad. And he'd have

loved you. He liked being around beautiful
women. (*Yawning contentedly.*) I wish I could
spend every day like this. You and me. In bed.
No timer.

KAMILA   Me too, Victor.

(*He looks at her thoughtfully.*)

VICTOR   Right. Good. I've got insurance on Joan's life.
Four hundred thousand.

KAMILA   Oh no, Victor. This is no good. I see it in
movie. It go wrong.

VICTOR   That's because the killer never waits long
enough. You take out a big policy and wham
bam the wife dies, they're bound to be
suspicious. I've had this policy six years.

KAMILA   You planned this good.

VICTOR   Yeah. A long time. I've got a secret savings
account in another name. My escape fund. I've
been stashing money in it since 1997. Bit by bit
by bit.

KAMILA   So? What will you do after?

VICTOR   Head off into the sunset with four hundred and
thirty-seven thousand quid. And, hopefully,
with you.

(*A moment. She freezes. He looks suddenly
vulnerable.*)

Don't say anything for a minute. I didn't know
what I'd do, after. Couldn't decide. I've been
waiting for a sign, I suppose . . . but it was
staring me in the face all the time. You. You're
the sign.

KAMILA	Now I know you're joking. You must be.
VICTOR	Why?
KAMILA	You? With me? You are Manager. I am . . .
VICTOR	You are beautiful, and generous, and kind. I want to look after you. You deserve better than this.
KAMILA	Serious?
VICTOR	Serious.
KAMILA	Wow.
	(*A moment.*)
VICTOR	You don't have anyone else, do you? Another man?
KAMILA	I am a hooker, Victor.
VICTOR	I don't mean that. I mean . . . anyone special.
KAMILA	Just you.
VICTOR	Oh Kamila.
KAMILA	(*after a moment*) I had a boyfriend before. Kaspar. Bastard. Russian, what do you expect? I ran away, came here, got a job.
VICTOR	And met me. Funny how life works.
KAMILA	Not so funny. (*A moment.*) You are mad. It won't work.
VICTOR	It will. A new start for both of us. A clean slate. I trust you.
KAMILA	Really? (*Touched.*) Really, Victor?
VICTOR	Yes.

KAMILA   We will spend the whole night together. For
               free, too. Can't wait.

VICTOR   I warn you, I snore. Joan says, (*Mimicking
               JOAN.*) "It's like sleeping with a sodding
               elephant."

KAMILA   (*laughing*) You are a crazy man. Crazy. I like
               it. Okay. We do it. We run off, happy ever
               after, much much sex. It's a nice idea.

VICTOR   It is, isn't it? A very nice idea.

               (*He turns round, grabs her, pushes her down
               on the bed. She squeals, laughing.*)

               So what can I get for forty quid?

               (*Blackout.*)

                            Scene Two

VICTOR'S *house. The dining table is laid for breakfast. The
radio is on quietly.* JOAN *is pouring hot water into the teapot
while simultaneously chatting on the phone.*

JOAN   I'm glad you called, Madge. I wanted to
               apologise for last night. You know what
               Victor's like when he gets going and Ted
               touched a bit of a nerve. He shouldn't have said
               that, I'm sorry . . . Look, I'll buy the wine next
               Saturday to apologise. I thought we might go
               Indian, that's Ted's fave, isn't it? . . . Oh. But
               we always . . . Oh, I see. The following week
               then . . . Ah . . .

               (VICTOR, *grumpy, comes in through the back
               door.*)

VICTOR   Every bloody time.

JOAN	Hang on a minute. (*To* VICTOR.) It's only a picture, there's no need to turn it into a drama.
VICTOR	I can't find the hammer.
JOAN	(*indicating*) In the kitchen drawer.
VICTOR	What's it doing in there?
JOAN	I used it on the outside tap when it froze. (*Into phone.*) Sorry about this.
VICTOR	Who's that?
JOAN	Madge.

(VICTOR *grunts.*)

(*into phone*) He sends his regards.

(VICTOR *opens the drawer and gets out a hammer.*)

VICTOR	Who keeps a hammer in a kitchen drawer?
JOAN	It got tidied away, that's all. It's not a hanging offence.
VICTOR	I've been looking for ten minutes.
JOAN	Just put the picture up, eh?

(*She picks up the teapot and goes into the living room, leaving* VICTOR *to hang the picture.*)

(*into the phone*) Are you still there? . . . It's okay, I get it, Madge, I really do. What? No, I hadn't heard. When? No!

(VICTOR *bangs a nail into the kitchen wall.*)

She must have been terrified. What did she do?

(VICTOR *bangs again, to* JOAN'S *irritation.*
Then he puts the hammer down on the side and
hangs a small picture.)

I'm not surprised. How old was this man? . . .
Typical, it's never George Clooney when you
want him, is it? I'll pop down and see her later,
poor thing. I'll get Victor to bake some of his
macaroons. That'll cheer her up.

(VICTOR *comes into the living room, sits at the*
table and reaches for some toast.)

JOAN   (*into phone*) What? (*With a glance at* VICTOR.)
              Too early to say. Yeah. Bye, love.

              (*She hangs up. They set about their breakfast.*)

              Madge.

VICTOR   You said.

JOAN   Have you had your insulin?

VICTOR   (*with a sigh*) Yes.

JOAN   I don't want to have to call an ambulance
              again.

VICTOR   I said yes.

JOAN   How does it look? My picture?

VICTOR   It's two fluffy kittens in a handbag. How do
              you think it looks?

JOAN   It makes me smile.

VICTOR   Yeah, well. This toast is cold.

JOAN   And good morning to you, my sweet.

              (*He grunts and picks up his paper.*)

	I had to go in the spare room again. I don't suppose you noticed.
VICTOR	I was asleep.
JOAN	Snoring your head off. It's like sleeping with a sodding elephant.
VICTOR	Mmm.
JOAN	It's not healthy having all those windows open. Germs blow in.
VICTOR	I can't sleep in a stuffy room.
JOAN	Well, I can't put up with cold air and draughts. We need a new bed in there, it's like sleeping on a park bench. The whole room's like a prison cell, it's that narrow.
VICTOR	It's not worth spending money on, is it?
JOAN	Course not. It's only me in there.

(VICTOR *doesn't react. He eats and reads.*)

Victor?

(*He still doesn't react.*)

Maureen had a tramp sleeping in her summerhouse. Madge just told me.

VICTOR	Which one's Maureen?
JOAN	Bottom of the hill. Green front door.
VICTOR	The one with the hips?
JOAN	Don't be unkind, she can't help it. Been living there for a week, apparently. Had a primus stove and everything.

VICTOR	I don't think you're allowed to call them tramps any more. I think the term is 'homeless persons'.
JOAN	He wasn't homeless. He lived in Maureen's shed. The police moved him on. I doubt he's gone far. He wasn't any trouble apparently. She felt almost sorry for him. He was only about your age. Sad, really.

(She waits for a reaction from behind the paper. Gets none. He does not reply. She eats. From behind his newspaper, VICTOR *starts quietly humming to himself. The Dam Busters March.)*

Victor. *(Getting no response.)* Victor!

(He stops humming. After a moment, he starts again. She grabs his paper.)

VICTOR	Hey.
JOAN	You're humming.
VICTOR	Was I?
JOAN	I swear you do it to annoy me.
VICTOR	I was thinking. I hum when I think.
JOAN	Does it have to be that? Can't you hum something more cheerful?
VICTOR	I like what I like.
JOAN	Don't I know it.

(She gets up, angry, starts to clear her breakfast things.)

VICTOR	I haven't finished.

(*She ignores him and takes things out to the kitchen. She looks at the newly hung picture and it cheers her up a little. In the living room,* VICTOR *starts to hum again.*)

JOAN   Victor!!

(*With a sigh,* VICTOR *folds his paper and, taking his tea, he makes for the settee. He picks up the remote and flicks on the TV (which is on the fourth wall). Dramatic music starts abruptly.* VICTOR *settles down to watch.* JOAN, *hearing the sound, returns to the kitchen doorway.*)

JOAN   You're not putting that on now.

VICTOR   I want to see how it ends. I was too tired last night.

JOAN   You know how it ends. You've seen it half a dozen times.

VICTOR   This is a new version. They might have changed it. They do that. There never used to be lesbians in Agatha Christie.

JOAN   Turn you on, does it?

VICTOR   (*annoyed, pausing the TV*) What's your problem?

JOAN   Oh nothing. It's Sunday morning. The sun's shining. What are we doing? Watching murder mysteries. Over and over. Not that I mind a good thriller.

VICTOR   The stuff you like is rubbish.

JOAN   Of course, it would be.

VICTOR	American trash. CSI, SVU, NCIS, it's all C-R-A-P, crap! They're not murder mysteries, they're cop shows. None of the great detectives is a policeman. They're independent investigators. Poirot, Miss Marple, Jessica Fletcher.
JOAN	Morse.
VICTOR	Morse doesn't count.
JOAN	You love Morse. He's a policeman.
VICTOR	The police procedural is a sub genre of which Morse, I grant you, happens to be the peak.
JOAN	Have you seen the old ones lately? They seem very slow now.
VICTOR	They're flawless. Absolutely flawless. Though even Morse isn't fit to touch the hem of the sage of Baker Street. The finest Sherlock of them all, the one and only Basil Rathbone. The Man.
JOAN	It was Jeremy Brett when I was growing up.
VICTOR	A bit poncey, Brett. Too much eyeliner. None of the new ones even begin to get it. Robert Downey Junior? All that druggy malarkey. Jonny Lee Miller with a female Watson? And as for that bloke on the BBC, Benedict Cucumber Patch . . .
JOAN	I like him. Nice little bum.
VICTOR	You can't judge a Sherlock Holmes on his bum.
JOAN	Don't see why not.
VICTOR	It's not a fair fight, for a start. It's modern dress. All the great Sherlocks wore frock coats, you never saw their bums.

JOAN   Pity.

VICTOR   (*realising*) You're deliberately winding me up, aren't you.

JOAN   I don't have to, Victor. I just light the blue touch paper and retire to a safe distance.

     (*Annoyed, he flicks the TV back on. He watches, pointedly.*)

JOAN   What is this, anyway?

VICTOR   One of Mrs Christie's. A particularly fine example too.

     (*She doesn't move. They watch. The soundtrack becomes lurid – a woman screaming, gurgling and whimpering piteously.*)

JOAN   What's up with her?

VICTOR   She's dying. Obviously.

JOAN   She's a bit dramatic about it.

VICTOR   That's what happens when you ingest cyanide.

JOAN   All that rolling around and whining.

VICTOR   Well, it hurts. Cyanide asphyxiates you from inside. Sucks all the oxygen out of you. Your face goes red, you gasp for air.

JOAN   Nasty.

VICTOR   Quick, though. An acute dose, anyway. Horrible agony, then death.

     (*A moment. The whimpering on the soundtrack stops.*)

JOAN   She isn't very convincing.

VICTOR	Penelope . . . what's-her-name, is one of our finest actresses. They should make her a dame.
JOAN	Over the top. Specially on that big screen.
VICTOR	Don't start.
JOAN	Takes up half the wall. I don't know why you bought it.
VICTOR	You had a new freezer.
JOAN	We'd had the old one since we were married!
VICTOR	Still had plenty of use left in it.
JOAN	Well, that's more than can be said for you.

(*Annoyed,* VICTOR *pauses the TV.*)

VICTOR	Can I watch this in peace or do you want a row?
JOAN	I don't want a row, it's Sunday. Why do you always pick fights on a Sunday? It's supposed to be a day of rest.
VICTOR	I don't pick fights.
JOAN	Every Sunday, like clockwork. I was telling Madge.
VICTOR	Oh great. I suppose all the neighbours know about my many failings, do they?
JOAN	No, just Madge. Although I might have mentioned it to Maureen.
VICTOR	Christ alive!
JOAN	You should be flattered. If I talk about you, I must still care, mustn't I? Oh, watch your programme.

VICTOR   You've spoiled it now.

         (*A moment. Neither of them knows how to bridge the gulf.* JOAN *starts to clear away the rest of the breakfast things.*)

JOAN   Are you going to do some baking? The tin's empty.

VICTOR   I wasn't planning on it.

JOAN   I could go for one of your bakewells. Or a stollen. Anything with almonds. Funny you should be such a whizz in the kitchen. Even Madge says you're good, and she's with the WI. She loves your macaroons.

VICTOR   I'll have that on my gravestone, shall I? "Here lies Victor Smiley. Madge loved his macaroons".

JOAN   Please yourself.

VICTOR   Mind you, you should lay off my macaroons. You could do with losing a few pounds.

JOAN   Victor!

VICTOR   (*remembering fondly*) You were lovely when I married you. Sleek, smooth thighs. Nice juicy bum. Tits like peaches.

JOAN   You weren't so bad yourself. (*Smiling.*) The worldly wise older man with a touch of the Roger Moore's. "He's a catch," I thought. (*Getting no response.*) I should have thrown you back.

VICTOR   (*the mood broken*) Here we go.

JOAN	I thought you were going places. Well, you did. A mile and a half up the A27. I thought you'd look after me, treat me nicely. Because you were older and wiser. But you were just older.
VICTOR	Let me know when you've finished.
JOAN	It never crossed my mind there was a reason no one else had snapped you up. God, I was naïve. You've fallen out with everyone we've ever met. You've even upset Ted.
VICTOR	When? He was okay last night.
JOAN	See? You've no idea.
VICTOR	He's a touchy sod.
JOAN	Specially when you compare his face to a baboon's scrotum. Fancy taking offence at that, the man must be mad. So that's it. The end of our Saturday nights out with Ted and Madge.
VICTOR	I say what I see.
JOAN	My life should be more than this.
VICTOR	What about mine? I thought we'd still be laughing together. I thought you'd still want wild sex three times a day.
JOAN	I do. Just not with you.
VICTOR	Ha! Sorry I'm not Johnny Depp.
JOAN	So am I, Victor. So. Am. I.

(*A moment. Then* JOAN *picks up her handbag, takes an envelope from it and thrusts it at him.*)

Happy Anniversary.

(*A moment. He is very taken aback. Rather sheepish, he opens the card and looks at it.*)

Fluffy kittens. (*Trying to be pleasant.*) It's nice, thank you. (*He has the grace to look uncomfortable.*) How long?

JOAN   Twenty years. Half my life.

VICTOR   Twenty years.

JOAN   If you say anything about time off for good behaviour now, you will regret it.

VICTOR   Twenty years. What anniversary's that?

JOAN   China.

VICTOR   Appropriate.

JOAN   Why?

VICTOR   We married each other. We're both mugs. (*A moment.*) Joke.

           (JOAN *looks desolate.*)

           We could go for a meal if you like. I've got a special voucher for Pizza Hut.

JOAN   Yes, there's nothing says I love you like a two for one meat feast.

VICTOR   There's that new place on Western Road.

JOAN   Mmm, why don't we? You can spend half an hour reading the menu then ask the waiter to explain the specials in detail. Then – oh, let me see – you'll order a prawn cocktail, steak and chips and a chocolate pudding.

VICTOR   When you go out for a meal, you want things you like. Things you don't get at home. (*After a moment.*) Pity they don't have sex on the menu.

JOAN   (*with a sigh*) You did that one last night, Victor. It wasn't funny then, either.

(*A moment.*)

You had such a spark about you when you were younger. You were tender. You'd look into my eyes when we made love, look right into me. When did that stop?

VICTOR   1997. It's like a blow.

JOAN   It wasn't just my fault.

VICTOR   You had hostile mucus. Nothing could grow.

JOAN   Your sperm count was low.

VICTOR   Real women don't need sixty five million sperm. One's enough.

JOAN   Most men have dicks that work.

VICTOR   That was a one off.

JOAN   So you said at the time. Famous last words.

(*Silence.*)

(*eventually*) God, I hate Sundays.

VICTOR   Well, so do I. But look on the bright side. They make Monday mornings something to look forward to.

(*He exits, leaving* JOAN *sitting there, utterly miserable. She picks up the anniversary card. Suddenly she perks up, newly animated, newly decisive.*)

JOAN   Right. Right!

(*Her face is full of purpose as she exits. Lights fade.*)

Scene Three

KAMILA'S *room. She is putting on mascara. A knock at her door.*

KAMILA   It's open.

                (ROY GRACE *pushes open the door.* GRACE *is late 20s, well put together, attractive.*)

GRACE   Ms Walcak? Kamila Walcak?

KAMILA   (*correcting the pronunciation*) Kameela. Not like the Duchess. Come in.

GRACE   Thank you.

KAMILA   Price list on the wall.

GRACE   You misunderstand me, Ms Walcak. I'm a police officer.

KAMILA   Okay. The usual, no charge.

GRACE   If you mean what I think you mean . . .

KAMILA   Don't worry.

GRACE   . . . you've just opened a can of worms I really don't want to get into. Ms Walcak, I'm not here for your professional services. And nor, I hope, are any of my colleagues. (*She shrugs.*) I'm looking for some information.

KAMILA   I don't know nothing.

GRACE   Let me be clear. You're not a suspect or in any danger.

KAMILA   Then what do you want?

GRACE   You were arrested at the end of last year, Ms
                  Walcak. For soliciting.

KAMILA   So? I work here now. I am not on the street.

GRACE   As I've said, you're not in any trouble. It was
                  me who arrested you. Do you remember?
                  Recognise me, maybe?

KAMILA   I don't look at men's faces much. (*After a
                  moment, looking at him.*) But you. But you . . .
                  you were not a bastard.

GRACE   (*ironic*) Thanks.

KAMILA   You were in uniform. You get promoted?

GRACE   Detective Constable Roy Grace of Surrey and
                  Sussex Police Major Crime Team.

KAMILA   Vice squad?

GRACE   Murder squad.

KAMILA   Murder? (*A moment.* KAMILA *looks at him,
                  suddenly wary.*) No.

GRACE   I think you might be able to help me.

KAMILA   Forget it.

GRACE   You came to us in February. You spoke to my
                  colleague, DC Hawkins.

KAMILA   He called me crazy. Called me mad bitch. So
                  no thanks, Mr Cop. Go away.

GRACE   I'm sorry DC Hawkins didn't listen to you.
                  What you said turned out to be right. I'd have
                  listened.

KAMILA   Yes?

(VICTOR *looks at her, still not getting it. Then he bends to his work. He starts to hum the Dam Busters March.*)

Victor!

VICTOR   (*looking up*) What? (*Seeing her face.*) Sorry.

(*He takes out a pack of cigars and lights one.*)

JOAN   Victor! We agreed you'd smoke outside.

VICTOR   You agreed. I didn't. And it's my name on the deeds.

JOAN   The smell gets in everything. It makes the paint go yellow.

(*He hums quietly, ignoring her.*)

It makes your breath stink too. You smell like a dragon.

VICTOR   You never used to mind. You said you loved my smoky breath.

JOAN   I said a lot of things. Doesn't mean I meant them.

(*He glares at her then goes back to the bills. After a moment . . .*)

VICTOR   It's your hair.

JOAN   At last.

VICTOR   It's on the credit card statement. A hundred and eighty five quid?

JOAN   That's very good for a cut, colour and extensions.

VICTOR	A hundred and eighty five quid?
JOAN	Take it out of the money I earn. (*After a moment.*) Do you like it? The colour's called Wild Raven.
VICTOR	(*looking at her, considering*) It's short.
JOAN	Yes.
VICTOR	It makes you look a bit butch.
JOAN	(*hurt*) Like you know what's fashionable.
VICTOR	Why do you need to be fashionable? You never go anywhere.
JOAN	Well, that's all about to change.
JOAN	I've decided to give something back. I'm going to contribute to the world.
VICTOR	What have you got to contribute?
JOAN	Charity work.
VICTOR	What sort of charity?
JOAN	I'm not sure. Breast cancer, maybe. Or maybe I'll volunteer at the Donkey sanctuary.
VICTOR	You don't give a toss about Donkeys.
JOAN	I must do, I married one.

(*He makes a face.*)

We were talking about it at work. The day Madge's car broke down and we had to share a taxi home. The cabbie gave us some ideas. Turns out he's very active in charitable circles.

JOAN	He said he'd introduce me to a few activities.
VICTOR	I expect he wanted a tip.
JOAN	He was rather dashing. He gave me his card. I might ring him.
VICTOR	Joan, I don't care if you douse yourself in paraffin and play with matches as long as you shut up and let me do the bills.
JOAN	Here we go. Another Sunday.
VICTOR	Oh, come on. We've always bickered. You like a good set to. You enjoy the cut and thrust.
JOAN	Not any more. Because, not to put too fine a point on it, Victor, there's too much cutting and not enough thrusting.

(VICTOR *tightens. He turns away from her.*)

Why won't you touch me anymore?

VICTOR	You're in the spare room half the time.
JOAN	That's not the reason.
VICTOR	I'm stressed at work. I've told you.
JOAN	See the doctor. He can give you pills.
VICTOR	I don't need pills.
JOAN	Victor, it's me. It's Joanie. You always said you could tell me anything. You still can.
VICTOR	Anything?
JOAN	Of course, anything at all. Or what's it all for?

(*A moment.* JOAN *thinks they're on the edge of a breakthrough. Maybe they are.*)

VICTOR   Do you know what I want, Joanie? Really, really want?

JOAN   Tell me.

              (*But* VICTOR *bottles it.*)

VICTOR   I want to do the bills.

              (*That's it. As far as* JOAN *is concerned, a rubicon has been crossed.*)

JOAN   Don't let me stop you.

              (*She goes to turn on the TV.*)

VICTOR   Can you not do that now please?

JOAN   I want to watch "Psychics Live."

VICTOR   I can't have the TV on while I'm working. Specially that rubbish. Ghosts don't exist. It's all smoke and mirrors, done for the cameras. And as for that psychic Malcolm, with the floppy hair . . .

JOAN   Sir Arthur Conan Doyle was a great believer in ghosts.

VICTOR   Sir Arthur Conan Doyle explored the subject according to rigorous scientific principles. He wasn't some anorexic ponce in yellow jeans and a face like Lily Savage. Can't you record it? You can gorge on it when you get home from stacking shelves.

              (JOAN, *conceding, operates the remote.*)

JOAN	It won't let me. You're already recording The Hound of the Baskervilles and Murderers Unmasked. Which one shall I cancel?
VICTOR	No, no, no. That's the Peter Cook and Dudley Moore Baskervilles. It's very rarely shown.
JOAN	The other one then.
VICTOR	You can't. It's about Dennis Nilsen.
JOAN	Which one was he? The heads in the fridge?
VICTOR	No, the one who flushed body parts down the bog. He was only caught when the drains got blocked and the plumber found human remains. Basic error.
JOAN	If I can't watch my programme now and I can't record it . . .
VICTOR	I said we should have got another telly. Not that ridiculous new freezer.

(*She looks at him. He goes back to his bills.*)

JOAN	I shall be out in the evenings a lot more from now on. On my charity work.
VICTOR	What will I eat?
JOAN	I'll take something out of that ridiculous new freezer. You won't starve.
VICTOR	You'll become a do-gooder. Everyone hates a do-gooder.
JOAN	It's healthy for couples to have separate interests.

(*He goes back to his bills.*)

VICTOR	What's this? "Karen Millen"? "L K Bennett"?
JOAN	I needed some clothes.
VICTOR	What's wrong with M&S?
JOAN	Where do you want me to start?
JOAN	If I'm going to meetings, I need to look smart.
VICTOR	(*looking at the bills, aghast*) Victoria's Secret?
JOAN	New underwear.
VICTOR	You're going to save Donkeys in expensive lingerie?
JOAN	The underwear was for you, Victor. For our anniversary. Remember?
VICTOR	(*not looking at her*) You'll have to send it back.
JOAN	It makes me feel good about myself.
VICTOR	I'm not paying for it.
JOAN	I work too.
VICTOR	Ten hours a week at Asda hardly compares with being the IT Manager for the ninth biggest egg box maker in England.
JOAN	(*oddly non-combative*) I'm sure you're right, Victor. (*He looks up at her suspiciously.*) What? I'm agreeing with you.
VICTOR	What's going on?
JOAN	Nothing, darling. Though I can see how it must look. New hair, new clothes, new lingerie. (VICTOR *starts to laugh.*) What?

VICTOR   You want me to think you're having an affair.

                (*He laughs even louder.* JOAN *is offended.*)

JOAN   I don't see what's funny about it. (*When he
                doesn't stop.*) I'm still attractive.

VICTOR   Yeah. But only to flies.

                (*He laughs. Upset, she gets up and walks past
                him into the kitchen. She snatches the cigar
                out of his hand and sticks it in her mug of tea.*
                VICTOR *continues to chortle as the lights fade.*)

                        Scene Five

KAMILA'S *room. A few days later.* GRACE *waits. After a moment*
KAMILA *enters comes in, with shopping bag.*

KAMILA   Oh.

GRACE   They said you were here. We found the boy.

KAMILA   Where I said?

GRACE   A small private mooring, west of here. He'd
                been wrapped up and weighted. We found him
                directly beneath the jetty.

KAMILA   Under boats, yes. You get the killer?

GRACE   We will. We found the murder weapon with the
                body.

KAMILA   Vajanje?

GRACE   Yes.

KAMILA   So. You find the body. Big success. You get
                gold star. Top of the class.

GRACE   Something like that.

KAMILA   Is your first case?

GRACE   Of course not. (*Then, a little sheepishly.*)
            Someone else's case, actually.

KAMILA   Ah. So now you look like the clever one. Now
            next time they give you one all of your own.
            All thanks to me. No?

            (GRACE *smiles. He doesn't contradict her.*)

GRACE   I wanted to ask . . . Would you consider being
            a . . . a sort of consultant? Not a relationship
            with the police, as such. A relationship with
            me. Confidential of course.

KAMILA   Oh, I get it. You want a relationship?

GRACE   Nothing like that, Ms Walcak. I could give you
            maybe a hundred pounds when your evidence
            leads somewhere.

KAMILA   So. You want to use me, Mr Cop. Same as a
            punter. Only a punter just wants my body. You
            want my soul. I don't ask to see. I don't want to
            see. And nobody believes me anyway.

GRACE   I believe you.

KAMILA   Why you different?

GRACE   I know things happen that defy science.

KAMILA   "Know", eh? How?

GRACE   It's not appropriate for me to tell you that.

KAMILA   Okay. Bye bye.

GRACE   Ms Walcak . . .

KAMILA   Kamila! Look, Mr Cop, you want me to trust
                  you? Tell me why I should.

                  (*A moment.*)

GRACE   Alright. When I was a little kid, I used to pass
                  this big old house near where we lived. There
                  were two old ladies who always sat in the
                  bay window on the top floor and they'd wave
                  every time they saw me. I always waved back.
                  A few years ago, when I went back to visit
                  my Dad, they were knocking the place down.
                  I mentioned the old ladies only to be told the
                  house had been empty for sixty years. There
                  had been two old ladies, sisters. One got cancer
                  and the other one decided she didn't want to
                  go on by herself. So they gassed themselves, in
                  that top room, sitting in the bay window. That
                  was in 1947. Years before I was born. Dad said
                  he and Mum had always thought the old ladies
                  were my imaginary friends. But they weren't
                  imaginary. I saw them. they were real. I don't
                  get whatever you call it, psychic flashes,
                  now, not as far as I know. But I don't dismiss
                  them in those who do. Does that answer your
                  question?

                  (*A moment.*)

KAMILA   Okay. I'll help you. Sometimes.

GRACE   Thank you.

                  (*He takes out his wallet and pulls out some
                  notes.*)

GRACE :   Here's a hundred. For the boy.

KAMILA   Hundred and fifty. I'm not a "tart with a heart"
                  on some TV show.

GRACE   Now listen . . .

KAMILA   No you listen, Mr Cop. You pay, you don't
                 pay, it makes no difference. I feel it anyway.
                 Bad sometimes. I go to a charity shop, buy a
                 scarf. Some dead old woman wants to send a
                 message. It's crap. I have my own life full of
                 crap, thanks. Don't need theirs. But it don't
                 stop them. So yes, money please. Why not?

                 (*He hands over another fifty pounds. She
                 counts it.*)

                 Good. You go now.

                 (GRACE *starts to go. Her voice stops him in the
                 doorway.*)

KAMILA   Don't mess me up. You do, I'll go to
                 newspaper. Tell them cop talks to mad Croat
                 whore.

GRACE   It's not really in your best interests to threaten
                 me, Ms Walcak.

KAMILA   Kamila. No threat. Just saying. You're okay, I
                 think.

GRACE   Yeah. I'm okay.

                 (*He goes.* KAMILA *looks after him thoughtfully.*)

                              Scene Six

VICTOR'S *house. The following Tuesday. In the bedroom, the
curtains are drawn. Two bodies are in bed.*

A deep snore from beneath the duvet. Then another. JOAN
pokes her head out from under the bedclothes.

JOAN   You're snoring.

(*She pokes him. He snores again.*)

Stop it. Stop snoring.

(*He wakes.*)

You're like a bear, a big growly bear.

(*She pulls the duvet away from him. He sits up. It's* DON – *a bit older, well preserved, fit, a bit of a silver fox.*)

DON   Was I snoring?

JOAN   Oh yes.

DON   Sorry. It drives Mandy nuts.

JOAN   I like it. It's sexy, like a teddy bear. A big cuddly teddy bear.

DON   (*in protest*) Cuddly? My abs are like rock, thank you.

JOAN   Come here, big boy. (*Snogging him.*) I never knew charity work could be so much fun.

           (DON *rolls on top of her and kisses her neck. She squirms.*)

DON   God, I love your body. I could drown in you.

JOAN   Any time.

           (*He buries his head between her breasts.*)

DON   Whoar!

JOAN   You don't think I'm . . . ?

DON   What?

JOAN	Fat? Over the hill?
DON	Rubbish. You're ripe, Joanie. Ripe, and sweet and oh so juicy.
JOAN	Don . . .
	(*They are about to get down to business again when an alarm clock goes off.*)
DON	Hell. Already?
JOAN	We could just . . .
DON	No, we can't. I've got the hospital run.
JOAN	We could if we're quick.
DON	It's a regular fare, I can't risk losing it. The council are good payers.
JOAN	Five minutes.
DON	But it won't be five minutes, will it, doll? More like twenty.
JOAN	Sounds okay to me.
DON	I can't be late, he freaks out. You know what old people are like.
JOAN	I bet I can change your mind.
DON	I bet you could. But it's my bread and butter. If I didn't have the regular runs for the council I couldn't spend my afternoons here giving you one.
JOAN	More than one.

DON   You're an enthusiast. It's what I love about
               you.(*He kisses her, then sits up.*) Chuck us me
               Alans.)

JOAN   Alans?

DON   Alan Whickers.

JOAN   Where are they?

DON   Wherever you ripped them off me.

               (JOAN *leans over the side of the bed and locates
               his pants. She dangles them in front of him.*)

JOAN   I want you every day. I wake up in the morning
               thinking about you. Your arms round me. Your
               weight on me.

DON   Stop it.

JOAN   You want it too. I know. It stands out a mile.

               (*Laughing, he extricates himself and gets
               dressed. She gets out of bed – in a black silk
               slip. She gets dressed too.*)

DON   Can you fit me in tomorrow, Mrs Smiley?

JOAN   (*giggling*) I'm sure I'll have an opening.

DON   You know what? It's seventeen years since my
               Sammi was born and Mandy went off the old
               zig-a-zagging. It feels like I've made up for
               lost time since I met you. We've had seventeen
               years' worth and more.

JOAN   Best month of my life.

               (*Both dressed now, they head downstairs.*)

DON	(*singing*) "Don't You Want Me Baby . . ." (*He hums some more outdated funky music.*)
JOAN	Don't hum, Don, eh?
DON	Sorry. I can't stop thinking about it. Sunshine.
JOAN	Swimming, shopping.
DON	Siestas. No more cabbying.
JOAN	No more Victor.
DON	You sure about it?
JOAN	Aren't you?
DON	'Course. Sammi's at college, nothing to stop here for. Let's do it nice, though, doll. No need to hurt him more than we have to.
JOAN	I thought you hated Victor.
DON	I do, he's a right Alphonse. I hate the way he neglects you. I hate how he makes his money.
JOAN	He's in paper products.
DON	Egg boxes. For battery hens. It's criminal, battery farming. He's got blood on his hands.
JOAN	I love it that you've got morals. You don't follow the herd. You think outside the box.
DON	Yeah. The egg box.
JOAN	I've given him that many chances.
DON	You've done your bit, gone the extra mile.
JOAN	You can't let your home be a battleground, can you? Not all the time. It's too tiring.

DON	Ours'll be a proper love nest. You, me and a king sized water bed.
JOAN	A real home. And maybe . . . No, it's too soon. You wouldn't want to, anyway.
DON	What? Have a baby?
JOAN	How did you . . . ? Forget I mentioned it. Of course you wouldn't.
DON	I'd love one. I love babies. All kids, really. Even teenagers.
JOAN	Really? 'Cause it might not be too late for me. It may not be straightforward, mind. Victor and I couldn't . . .

(*A moment*).

But they'll have made advances since then. It was all I ever wanted.

DON	We can give it a whirl, can't we? Anything that makes you happy. And we'll have fun trying, doll, trust me.

(*He tickles her. She laughs.*)

JOAN	First we have to get Victor out of our lives.
DON	You're sure we're doing the right thing? It is tough on Victor.
JOAN	It's the only way. Anything else, he'll dig his heels in. We have to clear out his bank account and jump on a plane. You're not backing out, are you?
DON	As if. (*Pecking her on the cheek.*) Got to go, sweet cheeks. Hasta Manana.

	(She kisses him goodbye. VICTOR'S *key is heard in the doorway.)*
JOAN	Jesus Christ. Kitchen, quick. C'mon Don. Quick. Out the back door.
	*(*DON *hurries through to the kitchen.* JOAN *adjusts herself as* VICTOR *comes in.)*
	Victor! What are you doing home so early?
VICTOR	Why shouldn't I come home?
JOAN	You're never home at this time of day.
VICTOR	Well, I am today, alright?
JOAN	Yes, but why? Why today?
VICTOR	I don't need the third degree, thank you.
JOAN	Please don't speak to me like that.
VICTOR	*(yelling)* How do want me to speak to you, you interfering cow?
JOAN	Victor!
	*(*DON, *heading out of the back door, hears the shouting and comes back in.)*
VICTOR	I don't need any backchat.
JOAN	Now you listen here . . .
	*(*DON *steps back into the living room.)*
DON	Is everything okay, Mrs Smiley?
	(A moment. Both VICTOR *and* JOAN *are surprised.)*

	Only I heard shouting and I was a bit concerned.
VICTOR	Who the hell are you? Joan? Who's this?
JOAN	It's er . . . He's . . .
DON	Ace Taxis, Mr Smiley. I've just brought your wife back from Rottingdean.
JOAN	(*thinking quickly*) That's right. It was an hour's wait for a bus. (*To* DON.) Thank you for bringing the shopping in. (*To* VICTOR.) The bag was really heavy.
VICTOR	Yeah, thanks. Don't let us keep you.
JOAN	Victor!
VICTOR	It's the last taxi you'll be getting for a while. (*To* DON.) Well, go on.
	(DON *can't think of an excuse to get her away. Then . . .*)
DON	Er . . . (*To* JOAN.) Seven pounds fifty.
JOAN	Yes. Yes of course. I'll get my bag.
	(*She leads him into the kitchen.* VICTOR *sinks down, head in hands.* DON *and* JOAN *have a whispered conversation.*)
	What on earth are you up to?
DON	Come away with me. Now. I'm not having you spoken to like that.
JOAN	It's nothing.

DON   It's not nothing. I won't have you bullied by
             that Strawberry.

JOAN   Strawberry?

DON   Split. Git.

JOAN   We've got a plan, we'll stick to it. Honestly,
             I'm not afraid of him. Go on, do your hospital
             run.

             (*She kisses him on the cheek and shows him
             out the back door. Then, girding her loins, she
             marches back in the living room.*)

             You do not speak to me like that, Victor
             Smiley, not in front of anyone else, not ever.
             Do you hear me? (*No response.*) Victor.

             (*Abruptly, to* JOAN'S *astonishment,* VICTOR
             bursts into tears.)

             Victor? What is it? What on earth's happened?
             Instinctively, she puts her arms round him. He
             allows it.

VICTOR   I'm glad you're here.

JOAN   (*surprised, touched*) Are you? Really? Victor,
             what's wrong?

VICTOR   I lost my job.

             (*A moment.* VICTOR *hugs her.* JOAN *stiffens.*)

JOAN   You're kidding.

VICTOR   I've been "let go".

JOAN   What did you do?

             (VICTOR *looks at her aghast.*)

VICTOR	Oh, that's it. Assume I did something wrong, why don't you? It couldn't be the recession or market forces or new technology. Or Stanley Smith and Son going down the tubes.
JOAN	Are they?
VICTOR	No.
JOAN	Well, then.
VICTOR	Mr Smith came in the office after lunch.
JOAN	Old Mr Smith?
VICTOR	No, the son. That fat twat Rodney. Sales are down, costs are up. Savings have to be found. I'm the saving.
JOAN	That's very short sighted of them.
VICTOR	Redundant. At my age. In this economy.
JOAN	You'll get money though? They'll pay you off.
VICTOR	Oh yes.
JOAN	Might be a nice lump sum.
VICTOR	The statutory minimum. A week and a half for every full year I've been at the company.
JOAN	Eighteen years.
VICTOR	Not till next month. He wants me gone by the end of this week. Four days notice, Joan. Four days.
JOAN	He can't do that.

VICTOR	He can do what he wants. So that's seventeen years. Twenty five and a half weeks pay. Plus the holiday I'm owed. Twenty seven weeks.
JOAN	Six months money. Only six months? That's nothing. That's nothing, Victor.
VICTOR	You think I don't know that?
JOAN	You should have made yourself more useful to them.
VICTOR	I can't believe you're going to make this my fault.
JOAN	What are you going to do?
VICTOR	We'll think of something.
JOAN	We?
VICTOR	We've got through worse.
JOAN	We were younger. Different people.
VICTOR	It'll do us good. A fresh start.
JOAN	I can't have you under my feet all day.
VICTOR	A clean slate. We'll have to pull our horns in, mind. I'll be cancelling your credit card.
JOAN	Over my dead body.
	(*A moment.* VICTOR *looks up at her as an idea crystallises.*)
VICTOR	Ha.
JOAN	What?
VICTOR	Nothing. Nothing at all.

JOAN	Victor . . .
VICTOR	I'm going to do some baking.
JOAN	Now?
VICTOR	Why not? A nice ginger sponge and some macaroons.

(He heads for the kitchen. JOAN *follows.)*

JOAN	Victor, we need to talk.
VICTOR	I'm thinking. Baking always helps me think. I've got plans to make.
JOAN	And what am I supposed to do? Spend hours stacking shelves while you watch bloody Poirot. Have you considered me at all?
VICTOR	You're always in my thoughts, Joan. You know that.
JOAN	Don't you dare get flour all over my kitchen.

*(*VICTOR *gets bowls, bags of flour, sugar, a bottle of almond essence etc, out of the cupboards. As he does so, he hums the Dam Busters March. Bemused,* JOAN *heads back into the living room. She gets her mobile and makes a call.)*

Don, change of plan.

(She hangs up. She calls to VICTOR.*)*

I'm going out.

*(*VICTOR *doesn't reply.* JOAN *goes.* VICTOR *arranges his ingredients on the side. As he gets to the middle of the Dam Busters March,*

*he stops. He has an idea. The Dam Busters
March starts again but this time, as he starts
with the 'dah dah dah', the humming turns to
a vocalisation. "Da-daahing" happily,* VICTOR
*goes out of the back door. We hear him still
singing as he opens the shed door, goes inside
and comes out again. He returns to the kitchen
with a dark green bottle in one hand and a
paper mask in the other. He puts the bottle on
the side as the Dam Busters March reaches its
climax. He puts on the mask. He picks up the
bottle. He hesitates as another thought strikes
him. He picks up the bottle of almond essence.
Blackout.)*

Scene Seven

KAMILA'S *room. Thursday. She lies on bed, rubbing cream into
a nasty bruise on her arm. After a moment or two, there is a
knock at the door.*

KAMILA   What?

                (VICTOR *opens the door. He is very cheerful.)*

VICTOR   Guess who.

KAMILA   Victor? It's not your day.

VICTOR   Oh, it is, Kamila. It will be. Very, very soon.

KAMILA   What's happened?

VICTOR   It's time. This weekend. (*Seeing she doesn't
                understand.)* Joan.

                (*He makes a throat cutting gesture.)*

KAMILA   For real?

VICTOR   Oh yes.

KAMILA	I thought it was what turned you on. Talking about it.
VICTOR	Maybe you're right. Maybe that's what it was. But not any more. You're still coming away with me, aren't you?
KAMILA	If you want.
VICTOR	Only I've had to bring my plans forward. Since I lost my job . . .
KAMILA	What? When?
VICTOR	Monday. It's my last day in the office tomorrow. But it doesn't matter, that's the beauty of it. I'm not rushing anything. I'm working it through, bit by bit by bit. That's what you learn when you study the masters. (*He rolls up his sleeve.*) Look. My tattoo.
KAMILA	WW8D?
VICTOR	WWSD.
KAMILA	What?
VICTOR	That's my motto. What. Would. Sherlock. Do?
KAMILA	Sherlock? Ah. I know. On TV.
VICTOR	That's right.
KAMILA	Man with nice bum.
VICTOR	He doesn't . . . Oh never mind. Well, my plan would outfox even him.
KAMILA	Tell me.

VICTOR   (*with pride*) This weekend . . . I'm going to paint the spare bedroom blue. (*A moment.*) You don't know how clever that is, do you?

KAMILA   Not really.

VICTOR   It's very small, our spare room. Smaller than this. Not much more than a cupboard, really. Joan goes in there when I snore. Sometimes I snore on purpose, just to piss her off. She never opens the window. She likes a fug.

KAMILA   Okay.

VICTOR   You ever heard of Prussian blue?

KAMILA   Russians are all pigs.

VICTOR   No, Prussian. With a P. Joan's favourite colour, as it goes. It's what they use to paint the Virgin Mary's cloak. Know what gives Prussian blue its colour?

KAMILA   No.

VICTOR   Cyanide. Now think back. What have I got in my shed?

KAMILA   Ah. I remember. How did you get it?

VICTOR   Work. There's a lot of chemicals in paper products. Cyanide's deadly if you ingest it. (*Seeing her incomprehension.*) Eat it, drink it. The vapour, the gas, that's even quicker. Course, there's not much cyanide in commercial paint, not these days. But if I mix my bottle in with it . . . See? The room gives off vapour as it dries. I snore my head off, my lovely wife goes next door to sleep . . . and Goodnight Vienna.

(*He is thrilled at his cleverness.*)

KAMILA   There's a problem. You'll die painting the
            room. The fumes.

VICTOR   I wear a mask and keep the windows open.
            When I discover the body, next morning,
            there'll be nothing for the cops to find. They
            can't trace who made the paint. They put it
            down to a fault in the manufacturing process.
            Terrible accident. I cash in the insurance and
            Bob's your uncle.

KAMILA   It might work.

VICTOR   No might about it. Anyway, I've got a back up
            plan. Belt and braces. I've kept a bit back, see?
            In this bottle of almond essence. Just in case.

KAMILA   Moj Bože.

            (*A little sheepish,* VICTOR *fishes something
            from his pocket.*)

VICTOR   Kamila, I hope you don't mind. I've bought
            you something.

            (*He hands her a jewellery box. She opens it. A
            moment.*)

KAMILA   Victor?

VICTOR   (*uncertain, like a little boy*) I hope you like it.

            (*She is touched.*)

KAMILA   Put it on me.

            (VICTOR *takes the gift from the box. It is a
            pendant, on a chain. He puts it round her neck.
            She fingers it.*)

            It's great. It's great, Victor.

VICTOR   It's a token, you see? A promise. Our future.

KAMILA   Thank you.

VICTOR   I'm going to treat you like a queen. Sweep you
                off your feet. (*Almost shy.*) I really need to kiss
                you, Kamila.

KAMILA   Okay. (*After a moment.*) No charge.

                (*Almost tenderly,* VICTOR *and* KAMILA *kiss.
                Lights fade on them.*)

Scene Eight

VICTOR'S *house. Friday night.* JOAN *is wearing a smart
wrapover dress. She clears away* VICTOR'S *plate from a dessert.
Hers remains uneaten. There is wine on the table, and a can of
beer.*

JOAN *takes the plate to the kitchen and gets another can of
beer from the fridge.*

The toilet flushes. VICTOR *returns to the living room, a little
drunk, doing up his flies.* JOAN *comes back in and hands him
the can of beer.*

JOAN   I thought you'd like another one.

VICTOR   Why not? Just this once.

BOTH   Cheers!

VICTOR   We're out of lavender spray in the downstairs
                loo. I'd give it five minutes if I was you. (*He
                burps.* JOAN *does not respond to any of this.*)
                That was a fantastic meal. Lovely bit of steak.
                (*Yawns.*)

JOAN   Just how you like it.

VICTOR   And the prawn cocktail. Beautiful sauce.

JOAN   I got the top of the range. I wanted to mark the
              day.

VICTOR   And that chocolate pud. Fantastic. Eat your
              heart out, Mary Berry. (*Seeing hers.*) Are you
              leaving yours?

JOAN   I'm stuffed. Fill your boots.

VICTOR   (*yawning*) Waste not want not. You are spoiling
              me tonight.

              (*He grabs it and starts eating greedily.* JOAN
              *continues to clear the table, taking salt and
              pepper, etc.*)

JOAN   You did take your insulin, didn't you?

VICTOR   Yes, but the food's all sugar free though, isn't
              it?

JOAN   Course it is. I used Canderelle. But use the
              pen again, eh? Just to be on the safe side. You
              know I worry. It's in the drawer.

              (VICTOR *injects himself again.* JOAN *returns.*)

VICTOR   Must have fallen out of my pocket. (*Yawning.*)
              You've done me proud. All my favourite
              things.

JOAN   Your last day at work. The life we've known is
              coming to an end, isn't it? We shouldn't ignore
              it. We should celebrate the good things. There
              have been good things, haven't there?

VICTOR   Mmm.

JOAN	I want to find a way forward. They say a problem is just an opportunity in disguise, don't they?
VICTOR	They do. (*Yawning.*) I'm feeling very positive about the future, as it goes.
JOAN	Me too.

(*He yawns.*)

VICTOR	(*incomprehensively*) I'm going to paint the spare room tomorrow.
JOAN	What?
VICTOR	I'm going to paint the spare room tomorrow.
JOAN	Really? After all these years?
VICTOR	I thought a nice blue.
JOAN	You hate blue.
VICTOR	But it's your favourite. It's the least you deserve. There's that one you love. Virgin Mary blue.
JOAN	Prussian blue.
VICTOR	That's the one. You can keep the window closed as much as you like.
JOAN	I'll sleep like a baby.
VICTOR	Yeah. Yeah, you will. (*Yawning.*) 'Scuse me, I must be tireder than I thought.

(*He goes to lean on the dining table but his elbow misses.*)

JOAN   You've had a stressful day. I know a good way
                to relieve stress. Remember that lingerie I
                bought? That you made all the fuss about? I'm
                wearing it now.

VICTOR   I feel a bit faint.

JOAN   Wait till you see it on. (VICTOR *grunts.*) Shall I
                show you?

                (*She undoes the front of her dress. She starts
                to shimmy. Then she starts to "La la" a
                seductive version of the Dam Busters March as
                she dances to the music.*)

                Come on, darling, it's your favourite.

                (*A bit bemused, overcome with sudden
                exhaustion,* VICTOR *tries to join with her
                singing but the sound is rather weak and
                feeble.*)

                Here's a little peek. (*She opens her dress
                facing upstage to* VICTOR.) Look how shiny the
                satin is. (*She approaches him.*) Don't you want
                to touch it, Victor? Don't you want to stroke it?

                (*She all but lap dances above his legs. Still to
                the tune of the Dam Busters March. It's bizarre
                but rather compelling.*)

                I'm naked under these clothes, Victor.

                (*As* VICTOR *reaches out towards her, she backs
                away, swaying seductively.* VICTOR *leans
                forward. And topples over. He falls to the floor
                at her feet. He doesn't move.*)

                Victor?

                (*No answer. She nudges him with her foot.
                Nothing. With sudden violence, she kicks him*

*in the crotch. He groans and sits up, opening
his eyes. She holds her breath. He falls back
again. A moment.)*

Victor? Oh dear, have we gone into a little
coma, sweetheart? Did naughty Joanie make
a mistake with the chocolate pud? Was it full
of sugar, after all? Naughty, naughty Joanie. I
know, let's give you some insulin, shall we?

*(She grabs the insulin pen off the table and
plunges it into his arm. And again.)*

Oh dear, doesn't seem to be working, does it?
Why's that, I wonder?

(Holding up the pen to the light.)

Ooh look. Did someone swap your insulin for
sugar water? Who'd do a naughty, naughty
thing like that, eh?

(The phone rings. JOAN *squeals and drops
the insulin pen. She looks around wildly then
lumbers to her feet and grabs the receiver. She
looks at the Caller Display.)*

(answering) Don? Madge! What a surprise! . . .
Breathless? Am I? Sorry, I'm just a bit . . . I've
been cooking Victor this special meal . . . Ah
. . . Sorry Madge, got to go. Something's come
up. As it were. *(Giggling.)* Victor . . .

*(She hangs up. Immediately her manner
changes. Her mobile phone receives a text
message. She checks it. Then goes into kitchen.
She gets a plastic bag and places the pudding
bowls inside it. Then she feels inside the
drawer and pulls out the hammer. She smashes
the bowls to pieces. Tentatively at first, then
with feeling, as if something is released in her.*

In the front room, VICTOR *groans. The back
door opens behind her.*)

DON   Joan?

(JOAN *drops the hammer into the drawer, then
takes a deep breath when she sees it's* DON.
*She deftly picks the RUBBER hammer up from
inside the same drawer.*)

DON   Have you done it?

JOAN   See for yourself.

(DON *goes to the doorway.*)

DON   Oh dear God. Is he . . . ?

JOAN   Well on his way.

DON   Houston, we've got a problem.

JOAN   What do you mean?

DON   I've been watching CSI with Mandy.

JOAN   Very domestic.

DON   Did you see it?

JOAN   No I was busy killing Victor, remember.

DON   It was about diabetics.

(*This gives* JOAN *pause.*)

It turns out quite a lot of diabetics have been
murdered by people giving them overdoses.
They have new ways of testing. You know,
forensics.

JOAN   Are you losing your nerve?

DON	'Course not, doll, I just . . .
JOAN	I researched this, remember? Victor's a Type One. Any Type One diabetic can go into a coma and die from too much sugar. I've had to call an ambulance for him more than once.
DON	So why didn't you call an ambulance tonight? That's what they'll ask.
JOAN	"I didn't know, officer? I was sleeping in the other room."
DON	They won't buy it.
JOAN	Of course they will.
DON	But CSI . . .
JOAN	CSI isn't real life.

(*A moment.* DON *wavers.*)

Look, all we have to do is tuck him up in bed and in the morning he'll be stone cold. I'll dial 999 and sob my little heart out but it'll be too late. Perfect, eh?

(*Still,* DON *hesitates.*)

Don, you promised me! Now come and help me get him up to bed.

(*They go into the living room and stare at* VICTOR.)

JOAN	You take his shoulders, I'll get his legs.

(*They prepare to pick him up. Just as* JOAN *is about to pick up his legs,* VICTOR'S *eyes open. With an incoherent cry he lumbers to his feet.*)

VICTOR   Ugh . . .

          (JOAN, *with a shriek, backs away as* VICTOR *lurches towards her.* DON *cries out.*)

JOAN   (*to* DON) Do something!

DON   Bloody Hell!

          (*She runs into the kitchen.* VICTOR, *realising there is someone else in the room, turns and sees* DON.)

VICTOR   You!

DON   (*panicking*) Taxi?

          (VICTOR *takes a step back towards him.*)

          (*In the kitchen,* JOAN, *panicky, looks around. She grabs the hammer from the countertop, walks back into the living room and swipes* VICTOR *round the head with it.*)

DON   Joan!

          (VICTOR *slumps down on the settee.*)

DON   Bloody hell.

          (JOAN *stands for a moment then bends over, retching, supporting herself on a dining chair.* DON *gapes.*)

          Bloody hell. Bloody hell. Bloody hell. Bloody . . .

JOAN   (*straightening up*) Will you shut up, Don! (*Taking a breath, then in wonder.*) It was so quick. One minute I've got a clean hammer in my hand, the next, abracadabra – I have a dead husband. Just like that.

(*She giggles.*)

DON   Well this is a sodding game changer.

JOAN   What shall we do with him?

DON   I don't know.

JOAN   Think.

DON   Oh Gawd, he's leaking on the sofa. Why'd you
             have to wallop him so hard?

JOAN   You'd have hit him softer, would you?

DON   Doll . . . This is probably not the best time for
             an argument.

             (JOAN, *decisive again, goes into the kitchen,
             opens a drawer and pulls out rubber gloves.
             She picks up the roll of bin liners and returns
             to* DON. *She hands him the gloves.*)

JOAN   Put these on.

DON   Pink?

             (*Seeing her look, he doesn't argue. She gives
             him a bin liner.*)

JOAN   Wrap him up. Stick a bag over his head. We
             can't let him drip. Forensics.

DON   You've bought them value bin bags haven't
             you. You need the heavy duty ones with the
             double draw strings.

JOAN   I'll remember that next time I'm disposing of a
             body.

(Trying not to look at what he is doing, DON slips a bag over his head. They both put his arms through holes they make. JOAN then makes a tube out of a bin bag for the torso, gives to DON.)

JOAN   Take this. Try folding it over.

DON   What? Have you done this before?

JOAN   Don, take it seriously.

DON   I'm wrapping your husband in bin bags. How much more serious could it be?

(They pull the tube bin bag over his legs up to torso level but can't completely fix in place until they stand him up later).

DON   Got any duct tape?

JOAN   Of course, I've got a whole serial killer kit in my handbag. (*Exasperated.*) Women don't have duct tape, Don.

DON   Parcel tape then? Sellotape? String?

(She rummages in the sideboard. Gets out a roll of duct tape. Holds it up.)

JOAN   Any good?

DON   Perfect. Now his legs. Come on, help me.

(He puts a bin bag over VICTOR's legs. JOAN wraps it in tape.)

DON   Eww. Do you think he's emptied his Simons?

JOAN   Simons?

DON   Simon Cowells.

JOAN   Don, this is not the time . . .

DON   Don't get the petrol.

JOAN   What?

DON   Pump . . . Hump. What is wrong with you?

JOAN   Just wrap him up will you!

            (*They lift* VICTOR *to his feet,* DON *holding him
            upright, pulling tube bin bag up to fully cover
            torso, whilst* JOAN *wraps duct tape round him
            to hold bags in place.*)

DON   What are we going to do with him?

JOAN   I don't know. I'll think of something.

DON   I saw this programme on the telly. They tried
            to dispose of a body in a bath of acid.

JOAN   Did it work?

DON   No, it melted the bath. Right bloody mess it
            was.

JOAN   Thanks for that Don, that's really helpful.

DON   I'm only saying . . .

            (*They place the body back on sofa.* DON *starts
            to wrap a bin bag around* VICTOR'S *left arm.*)

JOAN   Take his watch off. It's gold. No point letting it
            go to waste.

            (JOAN *places watch on sideboard. She places a
            bag over* VICTOR'S *right arm. Without taping it,
            she exits into kitchen.*)

DON   Where are you going?

JOAN   I'm thinking. You carry on.

DON   Thanks a bunch.

               (JOAN *goes back to the kitchen.* DON *tapes up*
               VICTOR'S *right arm. Quite quickly,* VICTOR'S
               body resembles a neat package. In the kitchen,
               JOAN *looks around for inspiration. Her eyes
               light on the chest freezer.*)

JOAN   Brilliant.

               (*She opens the lid and pulls out food. Three
               deep wire trays, crammed to the brim. Then
               individual bags and boxes from underneath.
               She piles them up on the floor.*)

               (*calling*) How you doing?

DON   Give me a minute.

               (*In the living room,* DON *finishes parcelling up*
               VICTOR.)

DON   Joan? (*Calling.*) Joan?

               (*Getting no reply, he goes to the kitchen. He
               sees the open freezer and all the food spread
               around.*)

               You absolute bloody star.

JOAN   For now. 'Til we think of something better.

DON   Right. (*Picking up a box.*) Ooh. Mini Kievs. Do
               you want to pop a couple in the oven for later,
               love? I'm starving.

JOAN   (*glaring*) Don. Get him.

               (DON *and* JOAN *go back to the living room.
               After a moment working out how best to handle
               it, they pick up* VICTOR'S *body.*)

DON   Jesus, he's heavy.

JOAN   He's had two puddings.

                (They manage to manoeuvre VICTOR *through
                the kitchen door.* DON *positions him over the
                chest freezer. They lower* VICTOR *into the
                freezer.* DON *slams down the lid of the freezer
                and forces it down. He and* JOAN *stand for a
                moment, grinning at one another.)*

JOAN   Right, come on.

                *(She marches back into the living room and
                investigates the settee.)*

                It's only this cushion, I think.

                *(She gets a bin bag and puts the cushion
                inside.)*

DON   Take your time. We don't want to leave any
                blood, or any . . .

JOAN   Any?

DON   Bits. Of anything. Fluids.

JOAN   We're going to say he's missing. They won't
                know it's a crime scene. And there'll be bits,
                as you put it, everywhere. We've lived here
                twenty years.

                (She thrusts the bag into DON's *hands.)*

DON   *(investigating the settee)* What's that? There.

JOAN   *(looking)* It's not blood.

DON   Do you think it's a bit of . . .

JOAN   What?

DON   Brain?

(They look at one another. She carefully picks it up between finger and thumb. She looks at it closely. Sniffs it. Then pops it in her mouth.)

Bloody Hell!

JOAN Cauliflower. He always was a messy eater. *(Straightening up.)* Right, you get off and dump that bag somewhere. I'll see you tomorrow. I'll clean up the kitchen. Go and pick up some fares. An alibi. Just in case. Give 'em a rant about foreigners or UFOs or something. So they remember you.

DON What about you, doll?

JOAN He's dead, isn't he? I'll be fine. Go on. I'm going to pour myself a large glass of wine and watch something I want on the telly for once.

DON If you're sure.

JOAN Don't fuss. Go on.

(She kisses him. Then she lets DON out of the back door and closes it behind him. She turns back into the kitchen. Her foot clips a tub of ice cream. She picks it up.)

Waste not want not.

(She gets a spoon. Heading back into the living room she pauses by the freezer.)

Like I said, Victor, it wasn't all bad, was it? I really enjoyed the last bit.

(She leaves the kitchen, turning off the light. A sudden noise outside. A clatter of bins, things falling.)

Hello? Hello?

(*She goes back to the kitchen doorway.
Tentative, rather spooked, she looks around
the kitchen. All is quiet. The sound comes
again.* JOAN *relaxes.*)

Damn foxes.

(*Taking the ice cream,* JOAN *heads for the
settee, picking up the wine bottle as she goes.
She turns off the main light, leaving just a pool
of light from the lamp. She settles down, picks
up the remote and turns on the TV. She flicks
channels.*)

Brilliant.

(*The only sources of light now are the pool
from the lamp by the settee and the light
coming in through the translucent blind at the
kitchen window. We hear the TV soundtrack.*)

TV   "I'm getting something, studio. I'm definitely
            getting something."

JOAN   'Course you are, Malcolm.

TV   "Yes, I have someone with me. Is there anyone
            here who has recently, very recently, lost
            someone called Victor?"

            (JOAN *freezes, horrified, staring at the TV. At
            the kitchen window, the silhouette of a man
            lurches into view.*)

            Blackout. End of Act One.

ACT TWO

Scene One

VICTOR'S *house. Saturday morning. The radio is on. There are several full bin bags piled on top of the chest freezer. Another bin bag, full of clothes, is by the back door.*

JOAN *is scrubbing at the kitchen surfaces determinedly. She is edgy and rather manic. The radio is playing "There May Be Trouble Ahead".* JOAN *is hardly listening at first, then the lyric starts to get to her. She clicks a button on the radio to change channels.*

Now it plays "Every Move You Make" by the Police. Abruptly, she snaps the radio off. She takes a deep breath to calm herself, then carries on.

[Note: Should rights to these songs be unavailable/expensive others can easily be substituted as long as the lyric reminds JOAN *of what she has done.]*

One of the bags slips off the freezer and thuds to the ground. JOAN, *adrenalin surging, spins round. She stares at the bag, then the freezer.*

JOAN   (*quietly, to reassure herself*) Come on, Joan. Everything's fine.

                (*When she is sure no more bags are going to move, she returns to her work. A hand appears at the glass of the kitchen door, knocks twice and disappears. Again,* JOAN *turns, startled. She takes a step towards the door, holding her breath.* DON *appears through the glass.* JOAN *exhales, noisily, exasperated, and opens the door.*)

DON   Morning.

JOAN   You scared me.

DON   Sorry, didn't mean to.

JOAN	It's open.
DON	I didn't know that, did I?
JOAN	You should have thought. Why do men never think?

(*She is agitated, close to tears.*)

DON	Hey. Hey, there.

(*He goes to embrace her.*)

JOAN	Don't touch me, leave me alone.
DON	What's wrong, doll?
JOAN	Take a wild guess. And don't call me 'doll'.

(DON *holds his hands up and backs off.*)

DON	You didn't sleep, did you?
JOAN	Did you?
DON	Yeah, actually.
JOAN	I thought I would, I took a pill. Two. I just got strung out. I had to take another one at four.
DON	You're bound to be upset. We did a big thing, Jack and Jilling him. Shall I put the kettle on?

(*During the following, he does so.*)

But we did it and it's done. As far as anyone knows, Victor's gone walkabout. That's all. No one has any reason to think anything else.

JOAN	You're right.
DON	We carry on like normal. You got a shift?
JOAN	Eleven till three. But I'm calling in sick.

DON	No, babe. Everything normal, like we said.
JOAN	I'm in no fit state to . . .
DON	Trust me, sweetcheeks. You can do this. Like the man said, when the going gets tough . . .

(*He puts teabags in mugs.*)

JOAN	Where did you park?
DON	Rodmell Avenue. I walked down from there.
JOAN	Good.
DON	You see, I do think.
JOAN	Sorry. I'm sorry, Don. I'm just . . .
DON	I know. Come here, sex bomb.

(*But she avoids his open arms.*)

JOAN	(*of the bag by the door*) That's everything I was wearing yesterday. You can take them to the tip. You should do the same with yours.
DON	(*indicating the bags on top of the freezer*) What's all these bags on the freezer?
JOAN	It's the food.
DON	Were you frightened he'd get out?
JOAN	What?
DON	Piled up like that. Looks like you thought he'd get out. You don't have to worry about that, dollface, he's Hovis.

(*A moment. She looks at him.*)

DON	Brown bread. Dead.

JOAN   I know what brown bread means.

DON   Dead as dead gets, doll.

JOAN   I told you, don't call me that. All this stuff you
            say, all the time. It's so phoney.

DON   Joan, baby . . .

JOAN   What? Do you want to take me up the "apples
            and pears"? Lay me down on the "Uncle
            Ned" and have a quick "Melvyn"? You're not
            a bloody Cockney, Don, you were born in
            Tunbridge Wells.

DON   Pembury, actually. Just outside.

JOAN   Oh hell.

            (*She bursts into tears.* DON *holds her, until she
            subsides.*)

DON   There. There, now. It'll soon be over. I know
            it's tough right now but just think about the
            future. Just keep your mind fixed on that. You
            and me on the Costas, free as air. Up to our
            arses in Cuba Libres. Forever and ever.

JOAN   Don . . .

DON   It's okay.

JOAN   It's not.

DON   So we'll make it okay. Okay?

JOAN   You don't understand.

DON   Course I do, doll, course I do.

JOAN   He was here. Last night.

            (*A moment.* DON *is wary.*)

DON	Who?
JOAN	Who do you think? Victor.
DON	(*after a moment*) That's not possible.
JOAN	I knew you'd say that.
DON	You must've imagined it.
JOAN	No, Don, I didn't. I did not imagine it.
DON	What happened?
JOAN	I watched some stupid programme on the telly, spooked myself a bit, I should have watched Corrie or something. I took a couple of pills and went to bed, tossed and turned for an hour. Then I smelt it.
DON	Smelt what?
JOAN	His cigar.
DON	Your nerves are shot, that's all.
JOAN	I came down here. The smell got stronger. I stood in that doorway and there he was, standing here, smoking a cigar, staring at me.
DON	Where?
JOAN	(*nodding towards the cooker*) There.
Don	(*instinctively, taking a step away*) Did he speak?
JOAN	No. Just stared. He didn't move or anything.
DON	Jesus, Joanie. What did you do?
JOAN	Ran upstairs and hid in the bathroom. Took another pill. Waited 'til dawn.
DON	You should have rung me.

JOAN	It was the middle of the night. Mandy might have answered.
DON	I should never have left you alone.
JOAN	No.
DON	I won't again.
JOAN	Good.
DON	Imagination's a funny thing.
JOAN	I didn't imagine it.
DON	Course you did. You must have done. (*Indicating the freezer.*) He's in the freezer isn't he?
JOAN	I suppose.
DON	You didn't check?
JOAN	I couldn't.
DON	Well, we'll soon see. (*He goes to the freezer, starts taking the bags off it.*) You want to keep this stuff. Put it back in, after.
JOAN	It's defrosted.
DON	Doesn't matter.
JOAN	We'll get food poisoning.
DON	We don't have to eat it, do we? Only it'll look weird if the freezer's empty.
JOAN	Who's going to look?
DON	Nobody.
JOAN	Why would someone look in the freezer if they just think Victor's missing?

DON	I'm just thinking ahead. Being careful.
JOAN	You think we're going to get caught.
DON	Course we won't.
JOAN	You said . . .
DON	We're not going to get caught. And even if we did . . .
JOAN	What?
DON	You were provoked, weren't you? Temporary insanity.
JOAN	I'm not taking the blame. Not by myself.
DON	I never said that, did I? Get a grip.
JOAN	We planned it together.
DON	And we'll get away with it together. Take a deep breath, girl.
	(*He moves the last bag. His hand goes to the freezer lid.*)
	Right.
	(*He hesitates.* JOAN *and* DON *look at one another for a moment.*)
JOAN	What if he's not there?
DON	Course he'll be there.
JOAN	What if he's not?
DON	Then we'll both be Donald Ducked. (*A moment.*) I love you.
JOAN	Me too.

(*Cautiously,* DON *opens the lid. He stares into the freezer for a long moment, expressionless.*)

Well?

DON   Jesus wept.

JOAN   (*scared*) What?

(*With his head,* DON *indicates she should come over and look for herself. Slowly, apprehensively, she does. Like* DON, *she stares into the freezer.*)

Oh Don.

(*Neither says a word. For as long as the moment will hold. Then a great grin spreads across* DON'S *face.*)

DON   See? What did I tell you? Not just brown bread. Total toast!

(*He slams the freezer lid down. With a little cry of happiness,* JOAN *throws her arms round* DON'S *neck. It's as though a floodgate has been opened. They start kissing one another, as if they will never stop.*)

Oh baby, baby . . .

JOAN   God I've missed you. (*Hands go inside clothes, belts are fumbled with.*) Yeah, yeah.

DON   I want you.

(DON *hoists* JOAN *up till she is perched on the freezer.*)

JOAN   What are you doing?

DON   You know exactly what I'm doing.

JOAN   We can't. Not here. Not with . . .

       (*He shuts her up by kissing her. She squirms.*)

JOAN   Don . . . (*His hand goes up her skirt. She
       gasps.*) Upstairs. Take me upstairs.

       (DON *lifts her up bodily. They are laughing
       and devouring one another in equal measure.
       She wraps her legs around him and he carries
       her through the house towards the stairs as the
       lights fade on them.*)

Scene Two

KAMILA's *room. The same morning.* KAMILA *enters, followed by*
GRACE.

KAMILA   I didn't think you'd get here so quick.

GRACE   I was on my way home. We arrested Ben's
         killer last night. Case closed, thanks to you.
         What's so urgent?

KAMILA   I'm frightened.

GRACE   Of what?

         (KAMILA *takes the small bottle of vodka from
         her pocket and swigs from it. She offers it to*
         GRACE.)

KAMILA   It's good. Polish.

GRACE   Just a small one.

         (*He takes the bottle and drinks a little.*)

KAMILA   You drink on duty?

GRACE   I'm not on duty. And it was a long night. So?

KAMILA	Promise to believe me, right?
GRACE	What about?
KAMILA	Promise.
GRACE	You haven't let me down so far.
KAMILA	Okay. (*Taking a deep breath.*) A man is dead.
GRACE	What man?
KAMILA	Name is Victor. He is my friend.
GRACE	Victor what?
KAMILA	You think men give second names here?
GRACE	He's a punter, then? You said friend.
KAMILA	He is a friend. Was. He was good to me.
GRACE	He's a regular? (*As she nods.*) When did you see him last?
KAMILA	Two days ago. Thursday. He gave me a present. (*She holds out the little pendant* VICTOR *gave her.*) It's nice. Not cheap. My neck won't go green.
GRACE	And before that?
KAMILA	Three times, each week. Long time. Same days. Like clockwork.
GRACE	And you think . . . ?
KAMILA	Feel. He is in a small space, dark. He screams.
GRACE	And he's dead?
KAMILA	Always they are dead. You must find him.
GRACE	I'll need a bit more to go on.
KAMILA	I don't know any more.

GRACE	You'll know more than you think. People always do. (*Of the pendant.*) Start with this. Why did he give it to you?
KAMILA	He said he loves me. He say we'll have a new life, him and me together.
GRACE	Does that happen a lot? With punters?
KAMILA	No.
GRACE	You said he was a regular. How long?
KAMILA	Six months. More.
GRACE	Does he live locally?
KAMILA	His work is near. He comes after, sometimes lunchtimes. He is manager of ET.
GRACE	IT? Information Technology.
KAMILA	Yes. Works in a paper place.
GRACE	Newsagent?
KAMILA	No. The company makes paper.
GRACE	That'll narrow it down. That's helpful, Kamila. Anything else? What does he look like?
KAMILA	Normal. I don't know.
GRACE	Hair?
KAMILA	Grey. Fair. Sort of.
GRACE	Long, short?
KAMILA	Normal. Kind eyes.
GRACE	What colour?
KAMILA	Blue. Not young.

GRACE   Over fifty?

KAMILA   I don't know, can't tell. I am useless, no?
             Stupid Croat whore.

GRACE   You're doing fine.

KAMILA   He is nice man. This is bad. Please. Believe
             me.

GRACE   I'll do my best. Leave it with me, I'll see what
             I can find out.

KAMILA   (*remembering*) He lost job. This week. He
             finished yesterday, Friday.

GRACE   You see? You do know things.

KAMILA   His wife is a bad woman. He tells me that a lot.

GRACE   I expect most of your punters say the same.

KAMILA   What do I know? Maybe his wife is okay.

             (GRACE'S *phone rings*.)

GRACE   Sorry, I have to take this. (*Answering*.) Hi
             Sandy . . . I had to make a stop on my way
             home, I'll be as quick as I can . . . Yes, me too
             Sandy. (*Hanging up*.) Did you feel anything
             else?

KAMILA   She took his watch. Before he died. Gold
             watch. White face.

GRACE   Okay. Maybe I'd better take some notes.

             (*He gets his notebook out as lights fade on
             them*.)

Scene Three

VICTOR'S *house. That afternoon. The back door is open.*

After a moment, we hear the front door close. JOAN *comes in from outside.*

JOAN	(*calling*) Don? Don, are you there?
	(*Getting no reply, she goes through to the kitchen, straight to the back door.*)
	What on earth are you doing?
	(DON *appears at the back door, in a sweaty T-shirt.*)
DON	I thought you'd be longer.
JOAN	Who's is that van in the drive?
DON	How did it go?
JOAN	Don, the van. Whose is it?
DON	Fret not. It's all hunky dory, I borrowed it off a mate.
JOAN	What for?
DON	I'll show you in a minute. Don't I get a kiss?
JOAN	You're all sweaty.
DON	I've been working hard. How did it go at the cop shop?
JOAN	It was fine.
DON	Honest?
JOAN	I went straight after my shift. I said my husband had gone missing, hadn't come to bed last night, was missing this morning.

DON   And?

JOAN   Didn't seem that bothered.

DON   They must have said something.

JOAN   They did actually. They asked if I'd tried
             calling his mobile.

             (*A moment, as the penny drops with* DON.)

DON   Bugger.

JOAN   Why didn't you think of that? Of course it's
             what I'd do. It's what anyone would do.

DON   You're right. Damn.

JOAN   How could you be so stupid?

DON   I had other things on my mind.

JOAN   What else didn't we think of?

DON   We'll sort it.

JOAN   It was all under control, you said. All planned.
             The perfect murder.

DON   It was a brilliant plan.

JOAN   Oh, really bloody perfect.

DON   It was till you bashed his skull in. (*A moment.*)
             Ring him now.

JOAN   Yeah. Okay.

DON   He's only missing. There's no harm done.

JOAN   He's on speed dial.

             (DON *hands her the phone. She presses the
             button.*)

DON   You'll get a shock if he answers.

> (*Glaring at him,* JOAN *walks into the living
> room as she waits for Voicemail to kick in.*
> DON *follows her to the door. On the sideboard,*
> VICTOR'S *phone rings. His distinctive ring
> tone – the Dam Busters March. Startled,*
> JOAN *hangs up. The ringing stops. Realising,*
> JOAN *grimaces at* DON *and redials. A moment.*
> VICTOR'S *phone rings again but this time she
> lets it. It stops of its own accord.* JOAN *closes
> her eyes, stands still for a moment, catching
> her breath. Abruptly, she hangs up.*)

Joanie? What is it?

JOAN   I wasn't expecting his voice.

> (*She sits down at the table, shaken.*)

DON   Whose voice were you expecting? Mickey
Mouse? (*Going for her phone.*) Look, I'll do it.

JOAN   (*grabbing it back*) You can't, can you? It has to
be me. (*She dials again.*)

DON   Put it on speaker.

> (JOAN *does so. We hear the ring tone. As*
> VICTOR'S *voice kicks in,* DON *takes* JOAN'S *hand
> and holds it. She is grateful.*)

VICTOR'S VOICE   Hello, this is Victor Smiley. You may have
deduced that I can't get to the phone right now.

DON   Too right, sunshine.

VICTOR'S VOICE   But if you leave a message I'll endeavour to
return your call.

> (*It bleeps.* JOAN *assumes what she considers a
> worried tone.*)

JOAN   Hello, Victor dear.

                (DON *looks at her questioningly. She waves him
                away.*)

                Where are you? Please call me, my darling. I
                am worried about you and I miss you so. (*After
                a moment.*) It's Joan, by the way.

                (*She hangs up.*)

DON   Who else would it be?

JOAN   Don't be picky. I was thinking on my feet.

DON   "Victor dear, I miss you so." Is that how you
                normally spoke to him?

JOAN   Yes, you're right. We should wipe it.

                (*She picks up* VICTOR'S *phone.* DON *grabs it.*)

DON   Don't be daft. He's supposed to have his phone
                with him. He can't wipe a message if he's dead,
                can he?

JOAN   I'm not thinking straight. You'd better dump
                his phone too. What else haven't we thought
                of?

DON   We mustn't panic.

JOAN   I need a drink.

DON   Come on, you'll like this. Let me show you.

JOAN   Don!

DON   Ta-daa!

                (*He takes her hand and leads her through the
                kitchen to the back door. He gestures through
                to the patio outside.*)

JOAN	What's this?
DON	What does it look like?
JOAN	A terrible idea.
DON	I'm a one man VDT.
JOAN	What?
DON	Victor Disposal Team.
JOAN	That's not funny.
DON	Come on, you're the one who wanted him offed.
JOAN	You're going to put him under the patio?
DON	That's what's in the van. All the tools. The big tub for the concrete.
JOAN	But the patio, Don. It's a bit Brookside.
DON	The garage floor's solid concrete.
JOAN	And it's broad daylight.
DON	You're not overlooked. If anyone asks you can say you're having a problem with the drains.
JOAN	That's what Dennis Nilsen said.
DON	Who?
JOAN	Never mind. You're not a builder.
DON	We'll get McAlpine's in, shall we?
JOAN	I'm only saying.
DON	I've done all sorts in my time. I'm good with my hands. As well you know.
JOAN	(*ignoring the innuendo*) It's not deep enough.

DON   I'm not finished. We'll put him down a good
           six feet.

JOAN   (*with a sigh*) Okay.

DON   Finish with concrete on top. I always did a nice
           screed. Then the old slabs back on top. Don't
           want the smell to start getting out when he
           decomposes.

           (*Reluctantly, she nods.*)

JOAN   I'll never be able to sell the house. Not with
           Victor out there.

DON   You can rent it out. Give us a nice little
           income.

JOAN   I suppose.

DON   "A well proportioned two-bed detached. With
           Downs views. And a well stocked garden."

           (*She doesn't want to be amused but she can't
           help herself.*)

JOAN   Shut up.

DON   That's better. We'll bury him tonight. After
           dark. To be on the safe side.

           (*The doorbell rings. They freeze.*)

           (*whispering*) Who's that?

JOAN   (*whispering back*) I don't know, do I?

DON   (*whispering*) Ignore it.

           (*They wait. The doorbell rings again. After a
           few moments, they relax. Then a knocking on
           the door.*)

JOAN	I have to get it.
DON	No you don't.
JOAN	My car's there, they'll know I'm in. Go in the garage.

(DON *heads out of the back door, out of sight.* JOAN *heads into the living room towards the front door. The bell rings again.*)

(*calling*) I'm coming. (*More knocks.*) I'm coming.

(*She goes into the hall. We hear the door open.*)

(*off*) Yes?

GRACE	(*off*) Mrs Joan Smiley?
JOAN	(*off*) Yes.
GRACE	(*off*) DC GRACE, Surrey and Sussex Police, Mrs Smiley. May I come in.
JOAN	(*off*) I, er . . . Yes, yes, go through.

(GRACE *enters the living room,* JOAN *following. She is completely thrown by this turn of events.*)

JOAN	Do sit down.
GRACE	(*not sitting down*) Detective Constable Roy Grace, Mrs Smiley. (*He hands her his card.*)
JOAN	Detective?
GRACE	Yes. We take missing persons very seriously, Mrs Smiley. The first few hours are critical. Most missing persons are found within a few days.

JOAN	That's a relief!
GRACE:	If they haven't turned up in thirty days, they've normally gone for good.
JOAN	(*trying to hide her glee*) Is that so?
GRACE	I wonder . . . Do you have a recent photograph? You didn't leave one at the station.
JOAN	I didn't think. Of course you'd want one.
GRACE	If it's convenient.
JOAN	We're not much for pictures. (*Looking around.*) Would this do? It's about five years old but he hasn't altered much. A bit thicker round the middle, perhaps. (*She hands him a framed photograph from the sideboard.*)
GRACE	Thanks. Normally, of course, this would be a matter for a uniformed officer.
JOAN	But I've got a Detective. Aren't I the lucky one?
GRACE	I take it you haven't heard from him?
JOAN	No.
GRACE	Of course, he's only been gone since this morning. So it's still early days.
JOAN	Seems like a lifetime.
GRACE	I'm sure. Is that your van outside, Mrs Smiley?
JOAN	Van?
GRACE	In your driveway.

JOAN   Oh, you mean the van. The white one. (*After a moment.*) Of course the white one, there is only the one, isn't there? The one van. Not as if there's room for two. Silly me.

                (*She realises that panic is making her say inappropriate things but doesn't know how to stop herself.*)

GRACE   Is it yours?

JOAN   Yes. I mean No. (*Thinking quickly.*) It's the plumber's van.

GRACE   Oh, dear. Trouble with the drains?

JOAN   Yes. (*Quickly.*) No. Nothing stuck down there. Nothing nasty. Nothing like that.

GRACE   Are you alright, Mrs Smiley?

JOAN   I'm fine. Well, worried, obviously. About Victor.

GRACE   Yes, of course.

JOAN   (*finding an explanation*) We're having the garage converted. Into a downstairs bathroom. Rather a large bathroom, obviously. We could have a party in it, it'll be so big. Not that we would, of course. Have a party in a bathroom. We're not . . . peculiar. Can I offer you a cup of tea?

GRACE   No thanks. He's very quiet, your plumber.

JOAN   Yes . . . He's deaf.

                (GRACE *looks at her in surprise. She could kick herself – but she just keeps digging.*)

From birth. We always use him, we know the
family. Poor man. Very very good. With pipes.
And things.

GRACE   Right.

JOAN   Good as gold. You wouldn't know he was here.

GRACE   Apart from the van outside.

JOAN   That's right.

             (*She smiles.*)

GRACE   I'm here, Mrs Smiley, because my colleagues
             in uniform have one or two concerns about
             your husband. Isn't it a bit soon to assume he's
             missing?

JOAN   Is it?

GRACE   He may simply have gone out for the day. Had
             an early appointment. Forgotten to tell you.

JOAN   Not Victor. He's . . . very regular. In his habits.

GRACE   I understand.

             (*A moment.* JOAN *waits to see if she is off the
             hook.*)

             Forgive me for asking, Mrs Smiley. But was
             everything okay between you? On the marital
             front?

JOAN   We adored each other. Ask anyone.

GRACE   We will. Yesterday evening was the last time
             you saw your husband, is that right?

JOAN   Yes. It was his last day at work. I told the other
             policeman that. Ever so upset, Victor was. I
             wasn't feeling very well. Nothing serious. A
             summer cold sort of thing.

(*Realising, she feels in her pocket for a tissue
and blows her nose.*)

GRACE   And you say he was upset after losing his job?

JOAN   Terrible. He was in shock. He'd given the best
years of his life to those sods. It destroyed
him, being let go like that. He was a broken
man. He sat here weeping, in this room, night
after night.

GRACE   Night after night?

JOAN   Since he was told they were letting him go.

GRACE   Which was?

JOAN   Monday. (*She realises she may have overstated
her case.*) When I say night after night . . . He
told me several times he didn't want to go on
living. He couldn't face not being wanted any
more. He was broken, totally broken.

GRACE   I telephoned Mr Rodney Smith earlier today.
Your husband's boss.

JOAN   Ungrateful so-and-so.

GRACE   He said your husband seemed glad it was his
last day. He told Mr Smith that he felt free for
the first time in his life.

JOAN   That's my Victor. Putting a brave face on
things.

GRACE   Do you have any insurance policies on your
husband's life, Mrs Smiley?

(*She is startled by the question.*)

JOAN   No. I Don't think so. Victor dealt with all that.

GRACE   Nothing you've taken out recently?

JOAN   No. What are you implying?

GRACE   Just a routine enquiry. We have to ask, you
               understand.

               (*A silence falls.*)

JOAN   Is that everything?

GRACE   For now.

JOAN   Right then. You'll . . . er . . . let me know?

GRACE   If we hear anything, yes.

JOAN   I'll show you out.

               (*She ushers him to the door. He stops.*)

GRACE   (*seeing it on the sideboard*) Is that your
               husband's watch, by any chance?

JOAN   Yes, yes it is.

GRACE   It's unusual. I like the white face. He left it
               behind?

JOAN   He must have done, I didn't notice.

GRACE   Does he usually leave his watch on the
               sideboard, Mrs Smiley?

JOAN   Er . . . I really don't know.

GRACE   I never take mine off. Or if I do, I put it on my
               bedside table.

JOAN   I don't know why he left it there. I don't know
               what he was thinking. Why he left. It's all a
               mystery.

GRACE   One I intend to solve. Thanks for your time.

(He is about to leave. The Dam Busters March starts to play as VICTOR'S *phone rings.)*

GRACE I can show myself out, Mrs Smiley, if you want to get that.

JOAN It's not mine.

GRACE Oh? Whose is it?

JOAN *(caught out, thinking fast)* It must be the plumber's, mustn't it?

GRACE Of course. Unusual ring tone.

JOAN Yes.

GRACE For a deaf man.

JOAN *(in agony)* People surprise you, Don't they?

GRACE Not policemen. Very little surprises us, I'm afraid. Goodbye for now, Mrs Smiley.

JOAN Goodbye, Inspector.

GRACE Constable.

JOAN Yes.

(And she has got GRACE *out of the door. We hear the front door close behind him. She hurries back into the room and goes to pick up* VICTOR'S *phone. She stops herself just in time. Waits. The phone stops ringing. She picks up the phone and checks the screen. Her head jerks up, suddenly alert. She sniffs. Smelling something, she looks around for the source of it. Her nose leads her to the hall door. She sniffs again. Steps back into the living room.)*

(calling) Don, have you been smoking in the house?

(*The hall door slams shut behind her. She turns, startled, spooked.*)

Don? Don?

(*She hurries through, almost breaking into a run as she heads for the back garden. Lights fade.*)

Scene Four

That night. It's dark outside. The kitchen, too, is in semi-darkness. The back door is open.

JOAN *and* DON *are there.* DON *opens the chest freezer. Light spills out, illuminating them.*

JOAN	There has to be somewhere else.
DON	Anywhere else is twice as risky.
JOAN	I know that detective suspected something.
DON	So?
JOAN	I don't think he believed we were happily married.
DON	Well, you weren't, were you? Or you wouldn't have put out for me.
JOAN	I did not put out. You seduced me.
DON	Yeah. (*With a grin.*) Yeah, I did. And if I'd known what I was getting into . . .
JOAN	(*taking it badly*) Oh, charming.
DON	(*taking her hand in his*) I wouldn't have done anything different.

(*A moment. She is touched.*)

JOAN   You don't mean that.

DON   You're my woman, Joanie. Don't you get that
                yet? My Brown Eyed Girl. My Lady In Red.
                The One That I Want. (*Singing.*) Ooh ooh ohh,
                honey.

JOAN   You're nuts. (*After a moment.*) Honest?

DON   Bet your arse, girl.

JOAN   I've always wanted someone to feel like that
                about me. Why didn't I meet you twenty years
                ago?

DON   Better late than never. Come on.

                (*He turns to the freezer, bends over it. Light
                catches his face eerily.*)

JOAN   We can't. I can't. I can't walk over him every
                day. We have to put him somewhere else. We
                can stick him in the van, drive somewhere. I
                don't know. Weigh him down and sink him
                in a lake. Loch Ness is deep, I saw it on
                Countryfile. If we leave now, we could be up
                there by morning.

DON   Trust me.

JOAN   I do, only . . .

DON   That's how murderers get caught, because
                a body turns up. If there's no body, there's
                nothing for the police to go on. It doesn't
                matter what that copper thinks or doesn't
                think. No body, no murder. Am I right or am I
                right?

JOAN   What if they come looking? What it they dig
                the patio up?

DON   Why would they? Victor's walked away from an unhappy marriage, that's all. Like Reggie Perrin. If that copper thinks you've been lying, that's what you've been lying about. That you were happy.

JOAN   (*reluctantly conceding*) Okay.

DON   So, give me a hand.

                 (*He bends into the chest freezer and reaches inside. He puts his arms around the body and hoists it out. It is exactly as we saw it before, still wrapped in bin liners.*)

                 Take the weight a minute.

                 (*Between them, they balance the body on the edge of the freezer.*)

                 Okay.

JOAN   He's harder than I expected.

DON   Not something you ever thought you'd say, eh doll?

JOAN   Don!

                 (*They manhandle the body to the floor. It slips out of* DON'S *hands.*)

JOAN   Careful.

DON   Ow! Bastard! (*He kicks the body.*)

JOAN   Hey! Show some respect.

DON   He landed on my foot.

                 (*A moment.*)

DON   What's up?

JOAN   I don't know. I suppose I thought I'd feel
            something. Sad. Or scared. Or guilty, or
            something. I thought I'd feel free.

DON   I know. Let's put the poor sod to rest.

            (*They drag him out of the door. A thump as
            he goes into the hole. After a moment,* JOAN
            *returns. She picks up the bin bags full of
            food and empties them into the freezer. A few
            minutes later,* DON *reappears.*)

            Okay?

JOAN   Yeah.

DON   You get to bed. I'll do the rest.

JOAN   But, I'll help you fill the hole in.

DON   No need. It'll only take an hour or so. I'll
            tamp it down and lay the screed. Concrete's all
            mixed.

JOAN   I don't mind. Won't Mandy be wondering
            where you are?

DON   I told her I've got an early pick up at Heathrow.
            Said I might pull an all nighter. Honest, doll,
            you'll be more a hindrance than a help.

JOAN   Okay.

DON   You go to bed. I'll be up soon as I'm done.

            (*He kisses her cheek. And keep your pecker
            up.*)

JOAN   Night.

DON   We'll crack a bottle of Cava in bed, eh?

JOAN   (*with little enthusiasm*) Lovely.

(DON *closes the back door. Heavily, weary,*
she closes the freezer, turns off the light in
the kitchen and heads into the living room.
Through the kitchen window, we see the
shadow on the blind of DON *filling in the*
hole on the patio. He maintains a steady
rhythm throughout the following. JOAN *crosses*
the living room. She stops. Looks round.
Suddenly spooked. Deciding she is being over-
imaginative, she turns back to the door. Now
we hear, quite distinctly, VICTOR *humming the*
Dam Busters March. She freezes.)

Don? Don, is that you?

(*The humming stops.*)

It's not funny, Don.

(*She goes back to the kitchen doorway. Seeing*
DON'S *shadow on the blind, she shakes her*
head as if to clear it.)

Silly.

(*She sets off back across the living room. As*
she passes the TV on the wall, it suddenly
bursts into life. A woman's voice, very loud,
sobbing and whimpering as she dies a horrible
death from cyanide poisoning. The soundtrack
we heard in Act One, scene two. JOAN *screams.*
She spins round. Staring at the TV in horror,
she scrabbles around on the settee for the
remote, unable to find it.)

Stop it. Stop, for God's sake.

(*She finds the remote, presses it, again and*
again but nothing happens – the awful sound
keeps on and on. JOAN *throws the remote at*
the TV. It makes no difference. Outside, DON
digs steadily on. Abruptly, the TV sound cuts
off. All we can hear now is JOAN'S *panicky*

breathing and the steady sound of DON'S
putting spadefuls of earth into the hole. JOAN
*runs into the hall, up the stairs, leaving the
door open behind her. A moment after she has
gone, the hall door slams shut, apparently of
its own accord.* JOAN *hurries into the bedroom,
shutting the door behind her. She pushes a
chair against the bedroom door and backs
away towards the bed, eyes glued to the door.
Nothing. Then, slow as slow, the door handle
turns.*)

Don? Don, is that you?

(*The door handle releases. She waits. Nothing.
For a long moment.* JOAN *whimpers. In the
kitchen,* DON'S *shadow continues its steady
rhythm. Just as* JOAN *starts to breathe again,
there are three gentle taps on the door.*)

Stop it. Go away.

(*A moment of silence. Then three more taps,
sharp now.*)

Please stop it.

(*More taps, faster, continuing on, not
stopping.*)

I'm sorry, okay? I'm sorry.

(*The knocking stops.*)

Victor? Don? (*Shouts.*) Don!

(DON *runs through back door to run up stairs.
The hall door slams behind him. On hearing
the door slam,* JOAN *pulls the chair away
from the door and, with bravado, pulls open
the door.* VICTOR *is there.* JOAN *screams. She
screams and screams and screams, unable
to stop. The door closes. With her scream*

*all the lights in the house come on, the TV
starts to blare its sound of death by poison
and the stereo kicks in playing at full blast
– a deafening cacophony.* DON *runs into the
bedroom.*)

DON   (*yelling*) Where's the fuse box?

                (*But she can't hear.*)

                (*yelling*) The fuse box!

JOAN   (*yelling back*) In the hall.

                (DON *hurries out of the bedroom. After a
                moment, the lights and the noise stop abruptly.
                All we hear now is* JOAN's *plaintive sobbing.*
                DON *comes back to the bedroom. He cradles*
                JOAN *in his arms.*

JOAN   It's Victor.

DON   It's okay. It's okay, doll, Don't worry. I'm here.
                Don's here. I'll look after you you. There now,
                baby. There now.

                (*Behind him, the bedroom door swings slowly
                shut.* DON *looks up, suddenly scared. We hear*
                VICTOR's *voice, quietly humming The Dam
                Busters March.* DON *puts his hands over* JOAN's
                ears, protectively. Blackout.)

                            Scene Five

Sunday morning. KAMILA's *room.* GRACE *and* KAMILA *are mid-
conversation.*

GRACE   Certainly Mrs Smiley was acting oddly,
                suspiciously even, but there's nothing that
                would alert us to a problem in the normal
                course of events.

KAMILA   It's murder. I know this.

GRACE	Try to see it from a police point of view. You say murder but we've nothing to suggest it's anything other than a missing persons case. Have you any idea how many people go missing every year?
KAMILA	You know I tell you true things.
GRACE	I'm not saying I don't believe you.
KAMILA	Then go and look. Victor is in the ground. Near house.
GRACE	I need good reason to search a house.
KAMILA	I'm good reason.
GRACE	The Chief Inspector won't see it like that. Victor's barely been missing twenty four hours.
KAMILA	I was right about the boy in the water.
GRACE	That was different.
KAMILA	(*upset*) Why?
GRACE	We were already investigating.
KAMILA	Victor is buried near house. Garden maybe.
GRACE	I need evidence to get a search warrant.
KAMILA	You can search if you make arrest. Arrest wife.
GRACE	I can't arrest anyone without reasonable suspicion. All I can do is ask Mrs Smiley some more questions.
KAMILA	So ask.

(*Agitated, she strikes out at his chest. He grabs her wrist to stop her.*)

GRACE   I will follow this up, Kamila, but I have to do
               it through the proper procedures.

               (*She subsides.*)

KAMILA   You bring in murderer, your first case, you are
               golden boy. No?

               (*He doesn't answer – but he doesn't deny it. He
               produces the photo* JOAN *gave him.*)

GRACE   This is your Victor?

KAMILA   Yes.

               (*She takes the photograph. Touches* VICTOR'S
               face.)

               You have wife? Girlfriend?

GRACE   I can't discuss my private life.

KAMILA   Boyfriend?

GRACE   No.

KAMILA   No loved one?

GRACE   Of course I have loved ones.

KAMILA   What if this was your loved one?

GRACE   Kamila . . .

KAMILA   It's mine. Victor is my loved one. The closest
               thing, anyway. He wanted to save me. Give
               me a new life. A future (*Touching the pendant
               round her neck.*) He called it a token. A
               promise. Now Victor's dead, I do what? Fifteen
               men every day till I am old? Great.

GRACE   There are other things you could do.

KAMILA   Sure. Work in pound shop.

GRACE   People do.

KAMILA   People do many things. People kill.

               (GRACE *doesn't answer.*)

               Wife and boyfriend killed Victor. Cut off his
               hands and head. Buried his body. I know this.
               For sure. You don't believe me, so no arrest.
               It's the perfect murder. Yes?

GRACE   I will investigate it personally.

KAMILA   Do what you like. I am finished. You go now.
               Don't come back.

GRACE   Kamila . . .

KAMILA   Piss off, Mr Cop. You're no good. Talk big but
               full of crap. Like all the rest.

               (*With a sigh,* GRACE *leaves.* KAMILA *looks after
               him. Lights fade.*)

Scene Six

A little later. VICTOR'S *house.* JOAN *sits in the living room,
motionless.* DON *comes in from the garden. He is subdued.*

DON   (*calling*) Joan? (*Getting no reply.*) Doll?

JOAN   I've told you not to call me that.

DON   Are you okay, babe? You look like hell.

JOAN   Boy, you really know how to make a girl feel
               special.

DON   Enough, okay? I'm trying my best here.

JOAN   (*after a moment*) Are you done out there?

DON	The slabs are down. It all looks good as new. So, yeah. We're hot to trot, babe. Free and clear.
	(*A moment. Neither of them knows what to say next.*)
	I should get out on the rank.
JOAN	Are we going to talk about it?
DON	We did.
JOAN	But you don't believe me, Don.
DON	It was late, we were spooked.
JOAN	It was Victor.
DON	It can't have been. It isn't possible.
JOAN	You think I made it up?
DON	I think we were both wound up.
JOAN	What about the TV? The lights?
DON	A fault or something. I don't know. I can't explain it, doll, I just know it can't have been that.
JOAN	I saw him.
DON	Well, I didn't.
JOAN	Not everyone sees ghosts. Maybe you're not sensitive.
DON	There's no such thing.
JOAN	A lot of people wouldn't agree with that.
DON	A lot of people believe in aliens. A lot of people think the CIA killed Kennedy. A lot

of people think Elvis runs a karaoke bar in
Swansea.

JOAN   I know what I saw.

DON   Your head was playing tricks.

JOAN   That's what he'd have said.

DON   What?

JOAN   You and Victor. You're exactly the same.

DON   Come off it.

JOAN   See? I say something you don't agree with,
            you dismiss it. Refuse to even think about it.
            Exactly like Victor.

DON   For God's sake . . .

JOAN   Something happens that doesn't fit your view
            of the world, you block it out. Deny it. He did
            that all the time.

DON   You're upset, I get it.

JOAN   Maybe it's all men. Maybe you're all the same
            under the skin. A woman said it so it must be
            crap. Don't take her seriously, God forbid, just
            nod and smile or she'll go all hysterical and
            refuse to put out. That's what men do, isn't it?

DON   No, we don't. That is crap, doll.

JOAN   So you said.

DON   Not because it's a woman saying it, but
            because it's . . . it's just crap.

JOAN   None of you can admit to being wrong, or
            out of control, or in over your head, or being
            bloody terrified. No, you always have to fix
            things.

DON	Calm down, eh?
JOAN	"Calm down, dear," is it? God!
DON	I'm nothing like Victor.
JOAN	'Course you are. Scratch the surface and there it is.
DON	Have you finished? (*Trying to change her mood.*) Come on, I'll take you for a drink. Get out of the house, blow the cobwebs away. Do us good.
JOAN	I saw Victor's ghost. He's still here, not just under the patio but here in the house. With us. He's angry. And I think he's going to haunt us for the rest of our lives.
DON	I believe you.
JOAN	You don't.
DON	I believe you believe it.
JOAN	What you mean is, "If I humour you, you might stop banging on and start banging me."
DON	I love you. I want us both to be happy.
JOAN	No. You want to be happy and you'll be more comfortable if I don't make a fuss.
DON	I don't know what to say to you.
JOAN	Then keep schtum. Quit while you're ahead.
DON	I don't feel like I'm ahead.
JOAN	You and Victor. Why didn't I see it? Was I just blown away by a bit of attention and a nice bum?

DON	Listen to me, you stupid tart. (DON *grabs her arm*.) I want to make a life with you. Got it? That's why I helped you kill Victor. I didn't do it for the sex, I can get that any time. And I don't give a toss about money, or Spain, or any of that. You lit up my life, you crazy bloody fabulous bloody cow, and I'd crawl over glass to stop you feeling the way you're obviously feeling now. But I don't, can't, won't, believe that Victor has come back to life and is wandering around with his head under his arm like Sir Walter bloody Raleigh. Because it's shit. It's just . . . shit.
	(*A moment.*)
JOAN	You're hurting me.
DON	(*letting her go*) Sorry.
JOAN	(*after a moment*) I think I would like that drink now.
DON	Where shall we go?
JOAN	You choose.
DON	The one on the Marina?
JOAN	It's a bit plastic. What about the bar at the Grand?
DON	That's pushing the boat out.
JOAN	Why not? Start as we mean to go on? Our new life.
DON	You never went there with Victor, did you?
JOAN	As if.
DON	Done deal, then.
JOAN	I can't go out like this. I look awful. You said so yourself.

DON   (*taking her in his arms*) You look like the
               woman I'm going to be sleeping next to for the
               next forty years.

JOAN   That's a bit optimistic.

DON   I am.

JOAN   I'll go and put my face on. You pop home,
               freshen up, see you up at four.

DON   I'll book us a room, too. You won't have to
               sleep in this house ever again. (*The phone
               rings.*) Leave it. We'll make it work, won't we?

JOAN   'Course we will.

               (*They kiss.* MADGE's *voice is heard on the
               answerphone.*)

MADGE'S VOICE Joan? It's Madge, love. We've had the police
               round. Why didn't you tell us Victor was
               missing? Why didn't you call?

JOAN   I'd better take this, she'll go on for hours.

               (DON *nods, pats her on the arm supportively
               and goes, closing the front door behind him.*)

MADGE'S VOICE I said to Ted, "I'm going straight round there.
               Poor thing'll be going out of her mind with
               fretting." Not that anything's happened to
               Victor, of course it hasn't. It's not as if . . .

               (JOAN *picks up the phone.*)

JOAN   It's alright, Madge, I'm here . . . Yes . . .
               Second day now. I know. . . . No, you don't
               need to worry, I'm sure he'll walk back in any
               minute . . . No, please don't bother. Really.

               (*The doorbell rings.*)

Oh, I've got to go, Madge, that's the door . . .
No, Victor wouldn't ring, would he? He'd have
his key . . . It'll be my plumber, he's only just
left, he'll have forgotten something.

(*The doorbell rings again.*)

Yes, thanks for calling, I appreciate it . . . Bye
now . . . Bye.

(*She goes into the hall, opens the door. A
murmur of voices.* GRACE *comes into the living
room,* JOAN *following.*)

GRACE   Good afternoon, Mrs Smiley.

JOAN   It's not very convenient, I was about to have a
          shower.

GRACE   It won't take long. A few things I'd like to
          discuss with you. One or two questions. Just
          routine.

JOAN   If you must.

GRACE   Is that your plumber I've just been talking
          to? He was just backing out of your drive as I
          arrived.

JOAN   No, it's . . . a friend. People are rallying round.
          Everyone's so worried about Victor.

GRACE   I thought it couldn't be your plumber. He
          wasn't in the least hard of hearing. (*A moment.*)
          Even though that's the same white van that was
          here yesterday. The one you told me belonged
          to your plumber.

JOAN   Is it?

GRACE   Can you explain that for me?

JOAN	(*after a moment*) No. No, I can't. You'll have to ask him that. My friend.
GRACE	His name being . . . ?
JOAN	Don. Kirk.
GRACE	Which one?
JOAN	Both. He's Don Kirk. Mr Kirk. People make jokes because he sounds like that place in France. Where the battle was.
GRACE	The van is registered to Mile Oak Electrical Services. They do plumbing as well, do they?
JOAN	I don't know anything about that. Why are you asking me about vans? Do you have any news about Victor?
GRACE	Bear with me, Mrs Smiley. When you filed the Missing Persons report, you said you'd rung your husband many times since he disappeared. Do you remember saying that?
JOAN	Yes, yes, I do.
GRACE	We've obtained your husband's mobile phone records and whilst there were a couple of calls from your landline to his. None at all from your mobile. The landline calls were placed yesterday, about an hour after you left the police station. Can you explain that?
JOAN	I tried him again, then. Yes.
GRACE	What about the other calls you say you made?
JOAN	There must be a mistake. I called him – I don't know – I don't know how many times. The phone company must have got it wrong.
GRACE	Does he have another phone, with a different number perhaps, that you've been calling?

JOAN	No, there's no other phone. I don't understand this.
GRACE	And his mobile phone is definitely missing?
JOAN	Definitely. He never went anywhere without it.
GRACE	I see.

(*He takes his phone from his pocket and dials. From inside the sideboard,* VICTOR'S *phone rings.*)

Is that your husband's phone, Mrs Smiley?

JOAN	(*in a tiny voice*) Yes.
GRACE	Would you get it for me please?

(*Uncomfortable, she retrieves the phone from the sideboard and hands it to* GRACE.)

How odd. And you were so definite.

JOAN	I must have made a mistake.
GRACE	Yes, I think you have. Because it rang yesterday, didn't it? While I was here.

(*A moment. Each waits for the other to speak.* JOAN *cracks first.*)

JOAN	I think I'd like a coffee. Can I get you anything, Inspector?
GRACE	Constable.

(JOAN *has scuttled away into the kitchen.* GRACE *follows. She is heading for the back door when* GRACE *asks, from the doorway.*)

The next thing I have to ask you about . . .

JOAN   (*glancing at the back door*) I'll only be
              a minute, Constable. Do make yourself
              comfortable in the living room.

GRACE   I'm fine here, thanks. I'm afraid this next
              question may be a little distressing.

JOAN   My husband's missing. I'm already distressed.

GRACE   Of course. Were you aware that he was
              planning to leave you?

              (*She turns to him, genuinely astonished.*)

JOAN   Victor?

GRACE   That he was having an affair?

JOAN   Don't be ridiculous, who on earth would –
              (*Stopping herself.*) I'm sorry, I . . . I don't
              believe that.

GRACE   Does the name Kamila Walcak mean anything
              to you?

JOAN   No.

GRACE   She rang your husband's mobile yesterday too.
              In fact, from the records, that must have been
              the call I witnessed. Do you remember that, at
              all? She withheld her number and didn't leave a
              message.

JOAN   Who is this woman? Why would she be
              interested in Victor?

GRACE   Miss Walcak is a sex worker in Brighton.

JOAN   A sex w . . . ? You mean a prostitute? He was
              paying for it?

GRACE   I'm afraid so, yes. He has been visiting her
              three times a week for almost nine months.

JOAN   (*furious*) Nine months! And he moaned about a
              few clothes. Bloody man.

GRACE   Miss Walcak claims she and your husband were
              planning to start a new life together.

JOAN   She must be mistaken.

GRACE   She identified Victor's photograph, without
              any doubt. Perhaps he has other women
              friends. Perhaps he is with one of them now.

JOAN   Maybe.

              (*She sees a way out.*)

              You could be right. I'm sure you are. I thought
              I knew him but . . . How well do we know
              anyone really? What they're capable of. I think
              you've got it. I bet he's with someone right
              now.

GRACE   Or perhaps you killed him.

              (*She stares at him.*)

              And buried him somewhere. Somewhere
              near the house, maybe? The back garden, for
              example. Might I look at your garden, Mrs
              Smiley? Do I have your permission?

JOAN   Why?

GRACE   Because I'm not satisfied with the answers
              you've given to some of my questions.

JOAN   Why would you think he's out there? That's a
              crazy thing to think.

GRACE   (*at the door*) Has your patio been disturbed
              recently? Some of the cement looks really quite
              fresh.

JOAN	So?
GRACE	Do you have something to hide?
JOAN	Of course not. I just don't see why you . . . (*She remembers something.*) You need a warrant to search my garden.
GRACE	Watch a lot of police shows, do you, Mrs Smiley?
JOAN	You can't look at anything without a warrant.
GRACE	I can if I arrest you. If I arrest you, we can search to our hearts' content.
JOAN	You've no reason to arrest me. You need grounds.
GRACE	You've lied to the police, Mrs Smiley. About the phone. Who knows what else?
JOAN	(*becoming upset*) You wouldn't. You can't.
GRACE	It would be better for you, Mrs Smiley, if you were to co-operate fully with our investigation.
	(*A moment. Then* JOAN *starts to cry.*)
	Mrs Smiley? Mrs Smiley?
JOAN	I couldn't stop him. He made me do it. He blackmailed me, threatened me. I was in fear of my life.
GRACE	Who, Mrs Smiley?
JOAN	Don. Don Kirk. (*Breaking down.*) He killed Victor with a hammer and made me help him hide the body. I've been going out of my mind.

GRACE   Joan Smiley, I am arresting you on suspicion of
               the murder of Victor Smiley.

               (JOAN *sobs and sobs as the lights start to fade.*)

               You do not have to say anything but it may
               harm your defence if you do not mention when
               questioned something which you later rely on
               in course. Anything you do say may be given
               in evidence . . .

               (*And the lights have gone.*)

Scene Seven

KAMILA'S *room. She comes in, taking off her outdoor coat and
throwing it on the bed. She bursts into tears. She pulls some
tissues from the box on the dressing table and sits down. She
opens the drawer and takes a swig from the bottle of vodka she
keeps there. Seeing her face in the mirror she groans and dabs
at her mascara with tissues.* GRACE *appears in the doorway.*

GRACE   It takes people like that sometimes. I'm sorry
               you're upset.

KAMILA   I pay extra for waterproof mascara. See? I look
               like a meerkat. The advertising lies. Everyone
               lies.

               (*She offers him the vodka bottle.*)

GRACE   I am on duty, this time.

KAMILA   I'm glad I went to court. Saw her face.

GRACE   Justice will be done, Kamila.

KAMILA   They should have locked her up not given her
               bail.

GRACE   She's only charged as an accessory to murder.
               She's been remanded to the Crown Court. She

will go down for what she's done, but I doubt she'll get long.

KAMILA   She doesn't deserve bail.

GRACE   She's not a flight risk or a danger to anyone else. She was coerced by her boyfriend, Don Kirk. All the evidence points to that. All the forensic. His DNA was found on the hammer. Which was in his car.

KAMILA   She should not have bail.

GRACE   It's the court's decision, not mine. And the gaols are pretty full. (*A moment.*) You haven't . . . felt anything else?

KAMILA   No.

GRACE   You've no idea where Victor's head and hands might be?

KAMILA   Sorry.

GRACE   I'm pretty sure his wife didn't know about that. She seemed genuinely shocked Don Kirk had mutilated the body. I suppose he thought it would make identification harder.

KAMILA   Did it?

GRACE   It would have once. Not these days. Victor had lived in that house for twenty years. We had hair from his comb, DNA from his toothbrush, pubic hairs in the shower tray. It all matched the DNA from the body. We didn't have to look very hard. Are you okay?

KAMILA   Maybe I go back to Croatia. I don't like this stupid country any more.

GRACE   I'm sorry to hear that. Is it better there?

KAMILA   No, not really. I was sad there. Now I'm sad
              here too. Very sad.

GRACE   Yeah. Murder's always sad.

KAMILA   Why murder is your career then?

GRACE   It's not my career. Solving it is. Preventing it.
              Getting the bad guys off the street, justice for
              the victims. Does that sound corny?

KAMILA   Honestly? Yes.

GRACE   (*liking her honesty*) Well. There you are. This
              was my first solo case. Thank you for helping
              me solve it.

              (*He takes out an envelope of money and offers
              to* KAMILA.)

KAMILA   No money this time. You are a good man Roy
              Grace. You will be great detective one day.

GRACE   You think?

KAMILA   Like Sherlock Holmes.

              (*A moment.* GRACE *senses something odd about
              her reply. She realises she has slipped up. The
              atmosphere tightens.*)

GRACE   Victor Smiley had a thing about Sherlock
              Holmes. There must have been a hundred
              DVDs in the sideboard.

KAMILA   Did he?

GRACE   He never mentioned it?

KAMILA   He never stopped. Poor Victor. While we were
              . . . Sherlock this, Sherlock that.

GRACE   Of course he did. Of course.

(*He seems to accept her explanation. A moment.*)

GRACE   'Til next time, then.

KAMILA   Make it a long time please.

GRACE   I'll do my best. And don't forget, if you do feel anything else . . .

KAMILA   I'll call.

(*He goes.* KAMILA *sits on the bed, gets out her phone and looks at it for a moment. Then she sends a text. Lights fade.*)

Scene Eight

VICTOR'S *house.* JOAN, *looking pale and wan, sits at the table, on the phone. A bottle of wine is open on the table.*

JOAN   Honestly, Madge, there's no need. I really appreciate your support – and please tell Ted the same. (*Tearful.*) I don't know that I deserve it.

              (*She listens, clearly irritated that* MADGE *won't stop talking.*)

              It's okay, I've ordered a pizza. There was nothing in the house, of course. Everything had gone off, I've been in custody so long. It won't be long. And I've found some of Victor's macaroons in the tin. They'll keep me going. Yes, something to remember him by.

              I can't explain it, the power he had over me. I was so stupid, if I could take it back, I would. Victor had his faults but I'd never have . . . No, right out of the blue. Swung at him with a hammer. Victor had just found out about Don and me, you see, and it was all . . . There was a lot of shouting, Madge, everyone was very . . . Don said . . . he said, if I didn't do everything he told me, every little thing, he'd kill me too . . . Yes. Look I've got to go, Madge. I'll call you in the morning. Thanks for everything. (*She hangs up.*) God she goes on.

(*She turns to see* VICTOR. *She screams.*)

VICTOR   I see you found the macaroons.

(JOAN *can't speak.*)

Don't worry, Joanie. I'm not a ghost.

JOAN   Victor?

VICTOR   Ghosts don't exist. They're just a trick of stupid people's minds.

(JOAN *throws her head back and is about to start screaming.* VICTOR *raises his arm. He has a crowbar in it.*)

Sssh, Joanie. Don't upset yourself. Eat your macaroon.

(*She looks down at the tin and up at him. He brandishes the crowbar. She takes a macaroon and nibbles at it.*)

That's my girl.

JOAN   I don't understand . . .

VICTOR   You never did, did you? It wasn't very understanding to wrap me up and put me in the freezer. Not without checking I was really dead.

(*He thrusts a writing pad and pen at her.*)

JOAN   What's this?

VICTOR   It's going to be your confession.

JOAN   I don't think so.

                (*He raises the crowbar. We think she will defy
                him for a moment, then she buckles.*)

                Alright, alright. What do you want me to say?

VICTOR   "Dear Detective . . ." What's his name again?

JOAN   Grace.

VICTOR   That's right. Good girl. "Dear Detective Grace,
                I hit my husband with the hammer." She
                writes. "I wish I hadn't. It was all my idea. I'm
                sorry."

                (*She looks up at him. They hold each other's
                gaze for a moment. Then she writes it.*)

                Sign it. (*She doesn't.*) Sign it! (*She does so.*)
                That'll do.

                (*He takes it from her and puts it on the table.*)

JOAN   I know about your whore.

VICTOR   I was unfaithful, yes. Not something you'd
                stoop to, of course.

JOAN   You drove me to it. (*After a moment.*) We put
                you in the freezer.

VICTOR   The freezer saved me. The cold woke me up. It
                took me a while to get out but I managed in the
                end. Bit by bit by bit. There was always a spare
                insulin pen in the kitchen drawer. I got myself
                straight. Well, straight enough. You saw me,

remember? I had a cigar and you were in the
bedroom and you came down and you saw me.
Or did you think you were dreaming?

JOAN   We buried you.

VICTOR   Obviously not. You see, I wasn't very happy
about what you'd done. You can understand
that, eh? I didn't intend for you to last the
night. I had a bottle of cyanide in the shed.
I thought, "I'll make her drink it, the bloody
bitch."

But I got lucky. Maybe the perfect murder
always needs a bit of luck. He was already
dead when I opened the shed door. The tramp.
Maureen's tramp, I suppose. I beg his pardon,
Maureen's homeless person. Dead as dead.
He'd opened all the jars and bottles. He must
have been looking for a quick high, meths or
something. He'd had the top off the bottle of
cyanide. It's very small, that shed. He hadn't
bothered putting it back on. The vapour had
done for him. I looked down at him and I
thought, "WWSD"?

JOAN   What?

VICTOR   "What would Sherlock do?" And then it came
to me. Have another macaroon, Joanie.

(*During the following,* JOAN *eats.*)

I got my comb and toothbrush from the
bathroom upstairs, combed his hair, cleaned
his revolting teeth, even put a handful of
his pubes down the plugholes. Just so as
everything would match, see?

I got the hacksaw and I cut off his head, then
his hands. Amazing how hard that was. Not
bloody, not so much – he was dead, there was

no blood flow. Just physically hard – not like
the TV at all. I wrapped him up in bin bags
and put him in the freezer instead of me.

Then I set about haunting you. Boo. You were
never very impressed with my IT skills, were
you? Never thought I was all that up to date.
It's amazing what you can do with wireless
technology and a remote control these days.

(*He goes towards her. She backs away. But
she's starting to feel dizzy.*)

Enjoying those macaroons, Joan? You always
loved almonds, didn't you? And there was an
extra special ingredient in the almond essence
for this batch. What else smells like almonds,
Joanie?

(*She looks down into the tin. Horror dawns on
her face.*)

God, you're slow sometimes.

(*She spits out the macaroon she has in her
mouth. But her legs go from under her and she
collapses, gasping.*)

I'm afraid I really must insist.

(*VICTOR kneels beside her, grabs her by the
throat and forces macaroons into her mouth.
He holds her mouth closed.*)

Swallow it, sweetheart.

(*Eyes bulging, face reddening, JOAN fights
back. She forces him away from her. She starts
to crawl across the room. VICTOR watches as
she collapses and starts to roll around on the
floor, gasping, choking.*)

Oh dear. Not very convincing, Joan. Not at all. You should learn from the masters.

(*He takes the TV remote from his pocket and flicks on the TV. We hear the soundtrack of the dying woman we heard in Act One, scene two.*)

That's better, Joanie. More gasping, less whimpering.

(*As* JOAN *writhes to her death,* VICTOR *watches dispassionately, comparing her death to the death on the TV screen. Finally,* JOAN *lies still.*)

Bravo, ladies. Bravo.

(VICTOR *clicks off the TV. He takes a phone from his pocket and dials. It is quickly answered.*)

(*into the phone*) All done. It's open.

He picks up the cake tin and puts the lid on.

As you said, our marriage wasn't all bad was it? I really loved that last bit.

(KAMILA *lets herself in through the back door, carrying two motorcycle helmets. Going into living room.* KAMILA *has a rucksack, turns so* VICTOR *can put in the biscuit tin and crowbar.*)

KAMILA   Sherlock would be proud.

(*He kisses her.*)

VICTOR   Thank God for you. You wound that young copper round your little finger.

KAMILA   Yes. But he is not a fool, Victor. The sooner we go, the better.

VICTOR   We'll be alright, you know. My escape fund
                will last a long time in Goa. I love you,
                Kamila.

KAMILA   I know you do. You made her write it? The
                confession?

VICTOR   Her suicide note. Yes. It's on the table.

KAMILA   And it's okay? Everything went okay?

                (VICTOR *takes out of his jacket pocket the*
                vanilla essence bottle of cyanide. Puts it by
                "suicide" note on table.)

VICTOR   Perfect.

                (*He turns off the living room light. They head*
                into kitchen. He turns off kitchen light. He and
                KAMILA *go, leaving the back door open, the*
                light from it just illuminating JOAN'S *motionless*
                body.)

                Blackout.